Creature Comforts

Wildlife Stories and Solutions

by Joel Thomas

Creature Comforts

This book is dedicated to my wife, Tracy, who for years has been telling me to *"write this stuff down."* For her support, for listening to my stories and pretending to be interested even when she wasn't. For still agreeing to sit in the boat when the fish weren't biting. For letting me hunt whenever and wherever I want. For not getting too aggravated at all the muddy boot tracks in the kitchen. And for always sending me out to the woods with a smile and having another one ready at the end of the day.

Trace, this book is for you.

Acknowledgments

It seems that sooner or later, behind any author, there accumulates a crowd of people he or she must thank. All, in one way or another, have contributed to this book, many unknowingly.

My thanks to the following people: To Dr. Bill O'Shea, for his encouragement, for catching the vision, for his technical expertise, and for being the first to convince me I could do all this. To Barbara Carr, for seeing something in me I didn't see. Thanks to Bev Jones for serving as an early sounding board. To Jan Schlegel, for being one of the first people that told me I could write. Special thanks must go to a team of volunteer editors. First, to Katie Rose for lending her laser-accurate editing skills to this project. Katie first opened my eyes to the need for sound editing. Connie Adams then lent additional eyes and valuable personal perspective to this project. Judy Meahl showed up and provided extra hands (literally) and finally Edith Bynum supplied the invaluable final copy editing. The absolutely terrific cover art and portrait photography were created by Joey and Jennifer Santora. And as dumb luck would have it, along the way Dr. Peter Freyburger suddenly appeared, to assist a great deal in the overall creation of this book. Thanks Doc!

And finally, to Bryan Meahl for long ago deciding to teach some kid how to hunt and fish. To my daughter Hannah, for checking in on me periodically to see if I needed a hug or anything. And to Jesus Christ who makes all things possible.

Foreword

There was a snort, a stamp, a threatening stare.
The buck had yet to learn
Of man and his destruction.
He filled his lungs with the forest air.
He bent to sip the virgin water.

This is wilderness.
Created by God.
Molded by Nature.
The province of wild creatures.
The far retreat of man.

As a veterinarian, I am anything but a poet. Nonetheless, I some-how managed to pen the first verse of the poem above as an assignment in junior high school in the mid-1960s. The second part was borrowed from a real poet whose name I have long since forgotten. Yet the poem itself has never left my mind.

At the time, it represented my idealistic view of the outdoors. And to be sure, it still does today, almost a half century later. Yet over the years, I gradually came to realize that wild animals are virtual-ly everywhere, if you just take a moment to look for them.

As you will soon discover in Creature Comforts, Joel Thomas learned that important lesson about wildlife at a much earlier age. No matter where we live, when we look out our back window, we often see wild critters. Some are obvious. Others are there only if we look hard. And a few are present that most of us will never see. Yet, rest assured, the majority of them see us.

No doubt most of us prefer to envision the deer in the poem above living in the wilderness. Yet in reality, he and many other wild animals have adapted to live in our backyards as well. And what many of us have forgotten is that our yards are often the wilderness of yesterday, and we are the actual intruders. The pages ahead will help us understand how we are all interconnected and how easy it can be for us to live together.

Ironically, today I live along the same creek in western New York where Joel spent his childhood and experienced many of the stories that are sprinkled throughout the pages ahead. While the number of houses has risen sharply since those days, the variety of wildlife has not diminished because that creek provides the water that makes everything in life possible.

In our backyard, there are year-round visitors such as squirrels, rabbits, flocks of geese, and a neighborhood red fox. Some animals make seasonal appearances. Lush grasses and available burrows along the bank of the creek attract woodchucks that show themselves to us in the summer. In the winter, snow transforms residential landscape plantings into a virtual salad bar, convincing deer to cross the highway when food is scarce and hunger trumps their usual preference for cover. Yet we rarely see the deer because they use the darkness as substitute cover and visit our plantings at night. We see evidence of their visits by fresh tracks traversing the yard after almost every snowfall. And last but not least, we spot infrequent visitors such as skunks, raccoons, small flocks of turkey, or even a rare meandering coyote.

All of these animals make their appearances if for no other reason than to enrich the lives and increase the sense of importance of our three family dogs. As a threesome, they try in vain to permanently evict each and every intruder. Surprisingly, a few wild animals elude even the watchful eyes of our pets. When I sit on our deck at sundown in the summer and watch high in the sky as twilight descends, a few bats almost always appear from places unknown to start their nightly mosquito patrol. I suspect some of our neighbors have no idea they are there, and perhaps it's better that way.

Over the past 30 years, my wife and I discovered that our interest in observing wildlife steadily transformed into a passion. We started out traveling to the usual exotic destinations like Africa. Before we knew it, we had moved on to the unusual places. We have had the incredible privilege to observe, in their natural habitat, wild animals that most people only see behind fences in zoos or on television nature documentaries. You might assume that, after having the unique opportunity to see everything from polar bears on the far north Arctic Tundra to penguins waddling across snow-covered rocks in Antarctica, backyard wildlife would become somewhat blasé. But you would be wrong. The more you learn about nature, the more fascinating it becomes. Noticing a red-tailed hawk perched in a cottonwood tree in our yard as it eyes a squirrel or hones in on songbirds near our birdfeeder is almost as fascinating as watching a brown bear in Alaska staring into flowing water watching for passing salmon. The process is the same. All of them are focused on survival regardless of whether they are the predator or the prey, the hunter or the hunted.

In today's modern world, far too many among us have lost the understanding of how wild animals interact with each other and with us. Through Joel's stories, you will soon find a better understanding of the critters that make appearances in your neighborhood. You will feel Joel's connection to those creatures. And before long, you will discover you enjoyed the process of learning, thanks to the sense of humor weaved into those tales. In the end, it will become easier to understand the behavior of wildlife after you are able to view the world through the eyes of the animals.

Fortunately, the vast majority of the time, local critters will live in perfect harmony with us and will entertain us as well, if we simply relax and allow them to do so. The secret is to find a way to react with less emotion than displayed by the typical family dog. The ability to use reason and understanding, rather than simply reacting with the same sense of territoriality as our canine friends, is the true reason we are our dog's masters. And on those rare occasions when a conflict of interest develops between you and any of the wildlife surrounding your home, Creature Comforts will be there on the bookshelf as a reference, ready to offer surprisingly simple solutions to what seems a difficult situation.

Peter J. Freyburger, DVM
Brighton-Eggert Animal Clinic
Tonawanda, New York

Contents

Prologue

I'm starting to regret not keeping a formal journal that would record almost 15 years in animal shelter work. As time goes by, you can easily convince yourself you have it all straight in your head. It's also tough to decide what people would want to read about. After awhile, what people with "normal jobs" would consider a complete, harrowing freak-out, most shelter workers tend to just shrug off and then go to lunch.

Punish the monkey, and let the organ grinder go...

Poochie, the Capuchin Monkey

Poochie had gotten a bad rap. A sentence he didn't deserve. He was innocent, but he did his time anyway. Confined to a small cell, Poochie did over 20 years. Poochie was a capuchin monkey—more commonly known as the organ-grinder monkey from a by gone era. As with many species of animals, people have a certain fascination with primates, monkeys and apes in particular. I've talked hundreds of people out of obtaining primates as pets. At least I think I have. The ones I haven't, by now, I'm sure, have learned that I was right. Any primate, no matter how large or small, is many times stronger for its size than it would seem. My rule of thumb: spider mon-key—breaks your finger; chimpanzee—breaks your arm, or worse. Combine great speed and strength with a level of intelligence that can make your smartest dog or dolphin look like an idiot, and you have a creature with which you do not want to share your life.

I forget the specific reason Poochie came to the shelter. But his owners couldn't, or wouldn't, care for him any longer. He had spent 20 years in a large dog crate, rarely if ever allowed any freedom. For me, the most striking feature of capuchins is their incredible canine teeth. The top two are over an inch long and when they want to show them, all four stick out. Way out.

The story goes that Poochie's owners would take the crate outside on sunny days so that he could get some fresh air. When they would return, there would often be bird feathers scattered around and inside the cage. For all his years in prison, this monkey wasn't feeble, or dumb.

The plan was to get the capuchin transferred to an acceptable primate sanctuary where he could live out the remainder of his years with a much higher quality of life. Before we could transfer him to his new home in Texas, at the request of the sanctuary, he would need a vasectomy. Neutering primates through removal of the sex organs is not advisable in colony settings as it puts the animals at odds with one another. Handling him directly was not practical or safe, and so, he was sedated in his cage. The operation went smoothly, once I found a veterinarian comfortable with performing the procedure. Primate vasectomy isn't on the average small animal hospital service list. Who knew?

Prologue

Poochie awoke in his cage none the worse for wear, with me being the last person he saw before the lights went out and the first person he saw upon waking up.

When the day came for his flight, he needed to be moved from the cage in which he had spent the last 20 years into a heavy-duty, well-constructed, lockable animal carrier. We all knew that if something were to go wrong, this was the perfect time for it to happen.

The room that we had kept the monkey in was a small room off a back hallway about 8 feet wide by 12 feet long. This setup gave him as much privacy as possible, while also keeping any contact with shelter staff to a minimum. Most primates are capable of carrying a host of human transmissible diseases. After enlisting the help of two rather reluctant assistants, I started by sliding the open shipping carrier up against the door of the monkey's cage and then removing the door to allow the monkey to enter the new carrier, hopefully in a futile attempt to escape. We would then close the door behind him and the transfer would be complete.

The monkey, as all the hipsters say, was not down with it.

Poochie remained crouched at the far end of his cage, staring into the abyss of the new carrier and showing no sign of moving whatsoever. Time for plan B. Looking back now, plan B needed to be filed under "it seemed like a good idea at the time". I hate that file. I suggested to my partners that we stand the two adjoining crates up on end, forcing the monkey to drop down into the shipping crate. Their enthusiasm was underwhelming. I was fairly positive it would work and if it didn't, there would be two grown men holding the two crates together, preventing the primate's escape.

We stood the crates up and, for a minute, nothing happened. Predictably, the capuchin clung to the sides of his cage to prevent himself from dropping down into unfamiliar territory. Suddenly he did just that—he dropped down into the shipping crate. Perfect, I thought to myself. Suddenly, with a show of unbelievable power and dexterity, the monkey reached up, took hold of his former home, and ripped it from our grasp. As he emerged from the shipping container, I felt a slight breeze behind me, which was generated by my two assistants evacuating the room at top speed. Before I could compute the situation fast enough to become afraid, a dark blur ricocheted off two walls and followed the path my two compadres had taken, out of the room and into the hallway.

The human mind is a marvelous computer. What separates us from machines is the ability of symphonic thought. Lots of stuff can flash through your head, all at once. There were several thoughts going on in mine as I headed out in pursuit of the fleeing primate. Where was he headed? How far would he get? Who might get hurt? What was the best way to explain this to my boss?

The two co-workers who had abandoned ship had apparently hung a left down the hallway. In the blink of an eye, the monkey had almost disappeared from my view. However, glancing to my right, I caught a flash of dark fur rounding the corner.

I knew then that I might get a chance to contain the hysteria that would ensue should this animal get loose in the shelter. The monkey had chosen a dead end. We had some routine capture equipment close by, as most animal shelters do. I passed on the common control stick, or pole snare, used by many of us. I knew from experience that should I get a chance to use it, the human-like dexterity of the monkey would make it very difficult to get anything over his head.

Instead I chose a device called a Freeman hammock net. This unique net had a flexible hoop made of carbon graphite and small mesh nylon netting terminating in a deep bag with an integral drawstring. This net could be used to contain anything from snakes to medium-sized mammals, and once in the net with the drawstring pulled, they were essentially in the bag, as it were.

I rounded the corner seconds after the wayward monkey and then stopped to see what he would do next. By then he had gotten to the end of the hallway, and luckily, the doors leading out were all closed. Though I wasn't exactly sure what his reaction to being cornered might be, I was hoping for a little cowering in fear, or perhaps some level of confusion on his part that could buy me some time. There was perhaps 25 feet of hallway separating us, and I readied the net as I took a step toward him.

Poochie, however, decided he wasn't going to cower in fear or remain confused. He looked me right in the eyes, and in that instant I knew he was coming. It was strange. It seemed we both knew that what he really wanted was just to get by me, and yet we both knew I couldn't let that happen. So he decided he was going to go through me if necessary. We squared off for just a second, and before he made his move, he showed me every one of his teeth. And what came out of his mouth was sort of a cross between a chuckle and a hiss. He took two short hops and was in the air arms stretched out in front of him and mouth open wide.

When I think back on what happened next, I remember it like an old western or action movie of the kind made famous by director Sam Peckinpah. In those movies, you could always count on some sort of intense, slow-motion action sequence. . For a more modern example, just think about the movie "The Matrix". We often function best by instinct, and this was one of those times. As the angry primate rocketed toward me, I made one quick swipe of the net across and in front of me, and much to the surprise of both of us, the monkey wound up directly in the bottom of the net bag. I pinned the hoop of the net to the ground and took advantage of the flexible graphite hoop, which allowed me to remain upright with the net bending flat to the floor.

By this time, my MIA co-workers had ventured back out into the hallway, saw that I had successfully gained control of things, and were readying the crate. Not wanting to risk losing control, I swiftly scooted him down the hallway floor and into the crate. The rest of the shipping process was uneventful, and Poochie was air freighted off to his new home. Every so often, I get a chance to talk to people who are totally enamored with the thought of keeping some sort of primate as a pet. Whenever that happens, I think of Poochie and I tell them this story.

Chapter 1 - **Why A Book?**

It seems as though, for most of my life, I have always been connected with animals in some way. I grew up in the 1960s and 1970s in East Amherst, New York, a suburb of Buffalo. As I was running barefoot through the fields, hunting and fishing, catching frogs in the neighbor's pond, and swimming in Tonawanda Creek it seemed natural for me. I didn't realize other kids grew up much differently until I hit junior high school. The few real friends I grew up with thought my interest in all things wild was kind of neat no matter what was currently living in my bedroom, and most of them never turned their nose up at whatever it was my mom was cooking in the kitchen.

Growing up, it never occurred to me what a gift this life might be.

The natural world was right outside our door. White-tailed deer, rabbits, squirrels, and pheasants were just some of the wildlife that lived around our home. We all enjoyed seeing wildlife. It was normal. It was a natural part of our lives. We watched, we learned, we took advantage of all nature had to offer, but we were never afraid of it.

Day after day, I see and speak to children and adults whose only perspective of and experience with wildlife come from watching the Discovery Channel. Observing pollywogs slowly growing legs and becoming frogs, finding a praying mantis that was hoping to stay invisible in the shrubbery, unraveling the tracks of some animal, or simply flipping over rocks and old boards to look for snakes or toads—these are all lost arts that I fear are fading away in exchange for video games, the Internet, and an unprecedented emphasis on team sports. Appreciating God's creation often takes some time, and most of us are willing to part with precious little of that.

Over the years I have realized that I am living in a world where most people not only do not know what creatures they share their own corner of the planet with, but also, in fact, do not know how to act or feel about them when the opportunity arises. This may seem strange to some folks—until they talk to the mother of young children who was terrified at the sight of a woodchuck in her back yard. Or, to the homeowner who was convinced that there shouldn't be rabbits in his neighborhood because he's never seen one here before. A raccoon, unlucky enough to be seen during the day, is often reason enough to form a posse.

One of my personal favorites is the conversation I had one day with a very irate woman who called me and wanted to know what could be done about all the noisy little frogs in her backyard. Now most of us, even those of us with concrete firmly under our feet, find the sound of spring peepers to be a pleasant harbinger of spring: a temporary, fleeting, musical chorus ending all too soon with the advance toward summer.

She, on the other hand, wanted those little buggers dead!

I gently tried to explain to her that it was a very temporary phenomenon, and that many people find the sounds soothing. She disagreed. She had "moved out to the country to get a little peace and quiet." We parted company while I pondered what could make someone hate these tiny, harmless amphibians, and while she considered draining all the standing water in sight of her property line.

I'm always fascinated by the interactions between people and animals. Sometimes, I think to myself, if I had the time, I should engage in some kind of formal study of the phenomenon. Then I come to my senses. Far too risky and much too dangerous. Not because of the animals; it's the people that scare me!

Although I teach people that they must be very careful using the words always, definitely, and never when dealing with animals, I have to say that at the end of the day, animals are way more predictable than most humans. Sometimes I think the reason why God made animals first and then man, was so man would not get scared out of his wits every time a new critter popped up in his backyard.

Often our human reaction toward wildlife is what I like to call "agenda driven." Humans are famous for agendas. We all have them, and just like our belly buttons, they are all different:

- Gardeners are suspicious of most rabbits.

- Rabbit lovers secretly wish that all animals who eat rabbits would die a slow painful death.

- Landscape enthusiasts constantly wonder why someone can't just come and "relocate" all the deer before they eat the shrubbery.

- Mrs. Smith down the street lets her toy poodle out every day and watches the sky, terrified that some owl or something will swoop down and carry off her little pooch.

- Mothers of small children fear anything larger than a songbird in their backyard. "I have young children here" is their mantra. (I regularly scan the papers looking for stories of small children being eaten by squirrels or turtles and yet, nothing.)

- Many hunters assume any animal with binocular vision that also hunts is competition, and so, needs to be wiped out.

- People who feed birds and squirrels in their backyards believe all hawks are the evil spawn of hell.

- Senior citizens are puzzling. They don't seem to need an unreasonable fear. Whatever it is, they just want it off their lawn.

But seriously folks, I kid my species. I'm a kidder. Through it all, I know there are times when legitimate conflicts do arise between people and wildlife. Wildlife, on the other hand, has only one agenda—survival. Wildlife isn't good or bad. Wildlife doesn't set out to make our lives more complicated. Wildlife will never show us gratitude when we help it or ask for mercy should we choose to harm it. Wildlife merely is.

This apparent disconnection, the misunderstandings people seem to have with wildlife, and my love for it generated the necessary inertia for this book. In it you will hopefully find some useful information: maybe some answers to wildlife related questions or problems, and perhaps, along the way, a little of me.

Author with his Fourth Grade Science Project

When it came to animals, I was blessed with patient parents. My mom was particularly laid-back about pets. As a matter of fact, she had a knack all of her own with critters. Her pets always seemed to set all kinds of longevity records: 10-year-old guinea pigs, 6-year-old hamsters, etc. She had a cat that, as far I know, was never sick a day in its life, lived to well over 20 years, and one day went outside, took a nap in the flowerbed and never woke up.

Throughout my teenage years I developed an interest in exotic reptiles. The exotic reptile trade was in its infancy back then. Not like today, when owning anything at all—big or small, short or tall, venomous or non-venomous—is limited only to the imagination and the strength of your Visa card. Yet somehow I still managed to acquire an impressive array of reptilian roommates. My mom seemed unflappable back then. I wonder now if some of the time I wasn't just trying to find her threshold of "are you *nuts*?"

She was even willing to help me care for them. As I got older and started working, she was okay with occasionally feeding something or changing a water dish. For years, one of my friends loved to tell and re-tell the story of hanging out in my bedroom/zoo one day, waiting for me to come home. I had this Tegu lizard. A Tegu is a carnivorous lizard from South America. Though known for their tameness, this was one of the nastiest creatures you'd ever want to meet. It spent much of its time in a cave at the end of a 6-foot-long enclosure. That is, until you went into the cage. Then it wanted a piece of you.

My friend was lounging in my room, checking out my menagerie, when my mom strolled in and, as was her custom, inquired if my friend was hungry and wanted a sandwich. As he turned to speak, my mother, noticing that once again the 2½-foot reptile had fouled its water dish, flipped open the top lid of the cage, which always caused the maniacal lizard to routinely burst forth from its lair with a display of hissing and charging the glass. Not pausing in her pleasant conversation with my friend, she grabbed the snake hook, and with a dexterity rivaling Marlin Perkins, pinned Godzilla securely behind the head and plucked the dirty water dish from the cage. Upon shutting the cage and promising to return with a snack, she left my somewhat speechless friend to his own devices, not only with a new-found respect for my mom but also with a great story we laughed about for years.

Early Starts

I think everyone who has an interest or hobby can think back to a time period, event, or distinctive moment that acted as a catalyst for them. We often don't even realize it at the time. In the mid-1960s, my oldest brother, James, enlisted in the Navy and very soon after wound up smack dab in the middle of the Vietnam War. As a member of an attack helicopter squadron known as the Sea Wolves, he was required to spend time in the jungle at remote air bases from which they would fly out on various missions, providing vital support for other units such as the Navy SEALS.

The way it was explained to me, jungle life in that region of Indochina wasn't exactly Jellystone Park. Rats, for example, could be quite large and unpleasant tent mates. The South Vietnamese remedy for this was to go down to the Mekong River, catch a python, and slide it under your tent platform. Evidently the large constrictors were often happy to stay there and avail themselves of the food supply that inevitably came in the night.

My brother hinted to us that he would be bringing some sort of surprise back home with him. We assumed something more conventional like a monkey, exotic bird, etc. Little did we suspect that he would stuff 9 feet of Indian Rock python into an AWOL bag and board a flight for home.

It was either really late or really early when my brother woke me up. I remember it being dark. I was 9 or 10 at the time. He took me out to the garage and there, coiled in a cardboard box, was the biggest snake I ever saw.

We knew nothing about caring for tropical reptiles back then. Practically no one did, except maybe zoos. This was decades before any real popularity in exotic reptiles and long before the Internet, export regulations, CITES (google this) lists, etc., so we just put it in a cage and fed it. Like many species of large constrictors, it ate quite readily, and it soon added 2 feet to its total length.

Ignorant of its needs for proper temperature, humidity, and such, we surprisingly kept it alive for a year or two. Upset at the death of the big snake, I began reading everything I could find on the subject of reptiles and their proper keeping. Looking back, being able to handle and observe such a large and unusual animal at an early age helped prepare me for other animal experiences later on. After handling 11 feet of python on a regular basis at 10 years old, there's not much else that really spooks you.

I grew up in a suburb of Buffalo called East Amherst. It is pretty suburbanized these days. However, 30 years ago, it qualified as the boonies. Today I drive by housing developments and strip malls that were the undeveloped brush and marshlands I hiked in as a young boy. Many of the animals that people ask me about today, I have enjoyed watching locally for years.

My home area of western New York, like many areas of the country, has seen much residential and commercial growth over the last 30 years. But with all the positive aspects that change can bring about, we are starting to see some of the negative aspects as they relate to people and wildlife. Early on in this process of growth, development was arguably a good thing for certain species; when land is cleared and open space is created, new plant growth can occur, making a favorable habitat. For example, white-tailed deer, contrary to what many people think, are creatures of open spaces and edges created when two forms of cover come together. Where your lawn meets uncleared brush, or a meadow stops at the edge of a woodlot is the type of place where you'll see deer because these transitional areas provide deer and other animals with food and cover. However, time marches on, and what we are experiencing now in many areas of our country is the wholesale loss of habitat due to suburban expansion and commercial growth.

Chapter 3 - **Habitat Modification**

Most of us spend a great deal of time and money keeping our property in good shape. While we regularly pay close attention to green lawns, landscaping, and fresh paint, these routine jobs of homeowners do little to prevent our wild friends from joining us in the house. Ironically 90 percent of unwanted wildlife encounters could be prevented by the installation of things like chimney caps, furnace vent caps, etc. If properly installed and maintained, these inexpensive devices last for years, preventing the unwanted entrance of many cavity-dwelling animals and birds.

The real key to any nuisance wildlife problem is habitat modification: the changing and manipulation of factors in the immediate environment that can change an animal's behavior. This aspect of dealing with nuisance wildlife is universal and only the methods change.

Wild animals exist, for the most part, on a delicate set of balance scales in terms of survival. The currency they have to barter with is energy. Energy stored and energy expended. It is what governs their movements, and it is their main weakness in our coming to an agreement with them.

Ninety-nine percent of the time it comes down to an energy trade-off. How much energy is the animal willing to expend in order to get what it is after? Finding that threshold and exceeding it is the main goal in abating a nuisance problem. The following is a list of the most common habitat related problems and easy modifications that can be utilized to quickly change the behavior of animals when conflicts arise. The main concept in these endeavors is exclusion. Exclusion can be done in many ways through the use of several different types of materials.

Chimney Caps

Chimney caps are simple, relatively inexpensive devices that fit over the tops of all kinds of chimneys and exhaust flues to prevent unwanted entry by birds and small mammals. Many homes have them. Many do not. Time and weather often degrade them to the point where they need to be replaced. This problem usually goes unnoticed until an unwanted animal gains entry into the building.

Dryer Vent Caps

Dryer vents that vent through a basement or wall are another hot spot for animal entry. Several different types of covers are commercially available and easy to install.

Roof Vents

This is another popular area of exploitation by wildlife. Designed to exhaust excess heat from the attic spaces of homes and commercial buildings, many of these types of vents have little thought given to their design or construction to exclude unwanted animal entry. When squirrels, for example, sense an exploitable cavity right on the other side of a flimsy piece of window screen, they will often invest the time and energy to work on it until they gain entry. Modifying these vents sometimes takes a little more skill than the average homeowner might possess. It often entails replacing the manufacturer's screen with a heavier gauge mesh such as ½-inch hardware cloth or welded wire. The best way to affix these materials to a metal roof vent is often with pop rivets. Though pop-rivets are available at most home improvement stores, some homeowners may choose to have these modifications done by a professional.

Sealants

It doesn't take much space for an unwanted entry to occur, particularly with small mammals such as rodents and bats. Caulking materials like latex and 100 percent silicone can be very effective and simple to use. Another useful product is expanding foam sealant. This polyurethane compound is applied under pressure, usually right out of an aerosol can, and quickly expands to fill most gaps that are too wide or irregular in shape for other conventional sealants. It is weatherproof, paintable, plus a good insulator. It can be used just about anywhere and is available at most hardware and home improvement stores.

Ground-Level Entry

Poorly fitting basement windows and gaps around electrical or plumbing service points are common problem areas. Window replacement and/or the use of sealants can solve most of these types of issues. Window wells can become traps for small or young mammals. Clear plastic window well covers not only solve this problem permanently but also provide a valuable thermal barrier to basement heat loss.

Denning Under Decks or Outbuildings

The outdoor deck is one of the most popular design features in modern architecture these days. Most of America enjoys the great outdoors high and dry, off the wet grass and out of the bug zone. The problem with much of deck construction is that it's designed with people in mind from the ground up. There is little thought about what happens when animals encounter it—until there is a problem. Most decks are designed to "float" over the ground, secured to vertical timbers anchored in the ground with concrete. These vertical posts are considered unattractive and are usually hidden underneath the decking. The finished product is an attractive deck that rides off the ground anywhere from 3 to 6 inches, which is just enough space to allow access to most skunks, woodchucks, raccoons, and opossums. These types of animals are constantly looking for cavities in which to live, breed, hunt, and travel through.

The wild skunk or gopher would choose the base of a large tree and locate its burrow among the root structure, deep in a hedgerow, or under a dead log. These types of cover are obviously scarce in the modern suburb, so wildlife is merely adapting to the changing landscape where it must live. The deck, porch, and stoop become the preferred cover of choice to protect the den.

Detached garages, storage sheds, pool cabanas, etc., are also favorite cover for burrows. All these types of structures can be animal proofed in one way or another by simply denying the animals access. The easiest and most cost-effective method is utilizing ½ inch metal mesh, or hardware cloth. This material is available at most large hardware or home improvement stores. The mesh is easily cut to size and then nailed or stapled to the outside perimeter of the structure, and either buried into the ground at least 6 to 8 inches or bent outward to form an L shape that lays on the ground. The horizontal leg can then be staked down and, if desired, landscaped over. Once secure in this fashion, the area is rendered permanently inaccessible to cavity-dwelling and burrowing animals.

Clutter

Another important aspect of habitat modification is the overall condition of our property and how it relates to animal behavior. Grass that is allowed to get too tall, excessive weed growth, clutter and debris, unused woodpiles, buildings in disrepair, and commercial dumpsters not serviced often enough are all major factors in the increase of nuisance wildlife problems in urban environments.

Modify the habitat to make it unattractive or unavailable to wildlife, and most problems will either disappear entirely or be reduced to a much more manageable level.

Birds

Territorial Issues

There are seasonal problems that can occur with some passerine, or perching birds. These issues revolve around nesting behavior and the territorial responses it can sometimes trigger.

Male songbirds often spend a great deal of energy defending their territory from rivals. This behavior becomes apparent when, for example, a male robin notices his reflection in the window and then relentlessly tries to drive off the "intruder."

Blocking the reflection and/or applying a distraction device can often eliminate this problem rather quickly. A piece of newspaper taped to the outside of the window where the bird is seeing its own image is one quick way to reduce the reflection. A colorful balloon tied or thumb tacked to the spot outside where it can move about in the wind can often distract the bird and make it wary enough to avoid approaching the spot. This method can also be used effectively for woodpeckers that occasionally begin drumming on the side of the house either in an attempt to drill for grubs or to communicate with other woodpeckers.

Adult songbirds can often be seen defending the nest site against any and all who approach. This behavior can take the fun out of having a family of robins nesting under the front stoop awning. Their defense is to scare and bluff anyone walking too close to the nest by flying around and dive bombing. This can be very disconcerting to many folks who are used to wildlife running the other way. The good news is the behavior is limited by the length of the nesting season, and the easiest abatement method is to use another door for a few days or simply to try and ignore all the fuss. Apparently Alfred Hitchcock has made it difficult for some of us to do that. Barring those options, if it's possible to move the nest away from human traffic a few feet at a time, many species, such as robins, are very tolerant of that. For example, my sister had a plant basket hanging from a shepherd hook outside her front door, and one day a robin built a nest in it. Not wanting to put up with all the fuss and yet not wishing any ill will on the frustrated bird, I simply suggested she pull up the hook, walk a few feet away from the porch, stick it back into the ground, and wait to see what would happen. A few minutes later, we watched the bird return and resume her place on the nest as if nothing had happened. By the same time the next afternoon, the hanging basket was well away from the front porch, the mother robin continued raising her brood in peace, and my sister had stopped doing her Tippi Heddren impressions.

Roosting Birds

The majority of roosting bird scenarios involves pigeons. The wild pigeon, or rock dove, can become a nuisance when it roosts in great numbers. Removing pigeons from a flock in an effort to reduce their numbers is usually unrewarding. Pigeons are tough, adaptable, year-round nesters that are here to stay. Living with them, once again involves habitat modification by taking away their roosting areas whenever possible.

One of the simplest ways to deny birds a roost is by stretching a wire or heavy gauge monofilament between two nails or spikes. The taught wire, running a few inches above where they would normally sit, more often than not causes them to move to another locale. This method can be utilized just about anywhere, from a windowsill, to along the ridgeline of any roof. Another method is to affix the wire in coils along a balcony rail or other area where roosting is occurring.

Deeper windowsills and the tops of window-mounted air conditioners can be fitted with shrouds, made of aluminum trim or sheet metal, that have a slope to them. This takes away the desirable flat surface that the birds sometimes prefer.

There are commercially available deterrent products such as bird spikes that are available in different lengths. These prefab strips can be simply mounted to any flat surface. The clusters of plastic spikes make it difficult for the birds to perch. The important concept here is to deny the birds the opportunity to roost.

Effigies can also be a useful aid in keeping some birds off balance and suspicious of roosting areas. The most effective being a large plastic owl. These are usually available at most large home and garden centers or through catalogs. The most important thing to remember with effigies is to periodically move them, or the resident birds will get used to them and they will rapidly lose their effectiveness.

Digging

A number of species can be responsible for digging. Gray squirrels, for example, are known to target flower beds in their effort to get at flower bulbs or bury food. Skunks favor digging in the lawn to get at the grubs that live in the grass roots. Chipmunks are usually busy expanding a tunnel network.

A great deal of digging in flower beds and landscape plantings can be discouraged through the use of hardware cloth or light gauge welded wire mesh. This product can be purchased by the foot at most large hardware stores and by the roll at any of the large home improvement centers. It comes in several mesh sizes; for this type of problem, choose the ½-inch size mesh.

Purchase enough to cover the desired area and cut it to any shape or contour with metal snips or heavy-duty shears. Plant your bulbs or seeds, lay the mesh down (pin it with a couple stakes if desired), and cover it with a thin layer of topsoil or mulch. The mesh remains hidden and out of sight, the plants come up through the ½ inch mesh, and when the squirrels attempt to dig, they are met with an impenetrable barrier. When digging proves unrewarding to the squirrels, they soon move on.

Grubbing activity by skunks can be a challenge and often depends on the tolerance level and attitude of the homeowner. As for me, I live in a relatively rural area and have over an acre of grass that I have to cut myself. I'm not just maintaining a lawn—I'm at war with the plant kingdom! If a few skunks want to periodically dig around in my yard and kill some grass, they are always welcome. Remember, if you have grubs and they get out of control, they will kill far more grass than the skunks will attempting to help you get rid of them.

Some folks want that perfect golf course look. My best advice to them would be to stay on top of any impending grub problems so as not to provide that food source to the skunks. When skunks begin grubbing activity, they often ignore other urban food sources in favor of the grubs. It has been my experience that the more manicured the lawn, the more vulnerable to grub activity it can be. We'll talk more about skunks later.

Fencing

There are many types of fencing: from low ornamental or border fencing that can help deter rabbits, to custom-made angled fencing designed to exclude deer or cattle. Attention must be given to what types of animals you're trying to exclude and to what abilities they have to defeat the barrier. Can the animals get under it? Over it? Through it? While these questions may seem so elementary as to not be worth mentioning, it has been my experience that they are often ignored.

These are some of the most basic and effective methods that are widely used for excluding wildlife from our homes and businesses. There are others. The important concept to remember here is making the space or habitat unattractive or permanently unavailable to the animal. Applying energy and resources here will always be more effective in solving or preventing conflicts.

Habitat modification, through direct exclusion techniques or landscaping, is the common thread that runs through our ability to live comfortably with wildlife.

The term nuisance wildlife can refer to any type of animal that is causing damage or annoyance by its presence on someone's property. Typically it often ends up being one of the many cavity-dwelling animals commonly found in one form or another all over the country. Squirrels, chipmunks, bats, raccoons, skunks, and woodchucks are the most frequent offenders when things go wrong.

I usually divide potential nuisance problems into two major categories:

Real, actual, nuisance wildlife situations

as opposed to

Perceived nuisance wildlife problems

A large majority of potential nuisance problems are solved merely with the right information. What animal is it? Why is it here? Is it dangerous? Often when these three questions are answered, the problem seems much smaller and way less scary.

Any animal that inhabits a structure by exploiting an opening of some kind and can cause physical damage to the structure through the course of its natural behavior is on its way to becoming a real nuisance wildlife animal.

Examples of this are squirrels and raccoons. Squirrels are some of nature's busiest creatures, as anyone who watches them can attest to. Squirrels need to store food, expand nest cavities, and make more squirrels. That's pretty much their agenda. In the course of their mission they often chew. They can chew wood, siding, insulation, and sometimes wiring. While I always discourage panic when someone discovers they have furry tenants, it is not a situation that I advise anyone to ignore.

Raccoons are, more often than not, just looking for a quiet place to bunk. The female wants a dark quiet nest cavity in which to raise her young. The male raccoon wants several locales to rotate in and out of in mild weather.

So what is the first course of action when we find we've been invaded? Intelligence gathering. Identifying the species is first on the list. This helps us plan a course of action that uses the animal's natural behavior to solve the problem quickly, safely, cheaply, and, most of the time, without causing serious harm to the animal.

Squirrels, raccoons, skunks, and woodchucks are all cavity-dwelling animals. One of the key facts to keep in mind when dealing with most cavity dwellers is that the female of the species usually has an alternate den site all ready, should she need to move her young. This is a potential key to resolving a problem.

When the presence of a female squirrel or raccoon is discovered, the first thing to begin thinking about is how to (a) expose the nest to the outside elements, and/or (b) manipulate the environment in others ways to make it less desirable to the animals.

For example, one day the maintenance supervisor where I work came to me with a problem. He was repairing the cupola on top of the barn. For the architecturally challenged, a cupola is the square little box-like structure with the pointed spire on top that adorns many traditionally designed structures such as barns and churches. Anyway, he related to me that when he removed a rotted piece off the side of the cupola, a gray squirrel suddenly burst from inside the structure, almost running him over as it tried to get away. After cautiously inspecting the inside of the structure, he discovered a leaf-lined nest with young, helpless baby squirrels.

By the look on his face as he gave me the details, I could plainly see that he fully expected me to get up there and "rescue" the young mammals because the mother was obviously gone, and he needed to finish his repairs to the barn roof. Suffice it to say that he was a bit puzzled when I said that wasn't our first course of action. I asked him to rip open the rest of the cupola, doing his best to expose the babies to the outside world, and then go get a cup of coffee. Ninety nine times out of one hundred, a female squirrel of any species will not tolerate her young being exposed to the elements and potential predators. If given the chance, she will immediately begin moving the babies to an alternate den site that she is already aware of.

Take care to try and eliminate commotion and human presence around the den site until the female squirrel feels at ease enough to begin moving her brood. It's a process that can take a couple hours, so patience is the key. Homeowners and contractors are often resistant to the idea of stopping in the middle of repairs to allow the animal's natural behavior to kick in. Most people's natural reaction is to call someone to remove, or get rid, of the troublesome critter. Curiously, these are often the same people that usually go nuts when someone wants to charge them for animal removal. (By the way, the maintenance supervisor came and found me an hour and a half later to say all the baby squirrels were gone.)

When it isn't practical or possible to expose a den site, the next course of action is to try and illuminate the dark nest area. This can be accomplished with an extension cord and work light or light bulb fixture. In addition to light, loud music can help accelerate the process. This works great for raccoons who usually end up somewhere in the eaves, where exposing them isn't practical.

A family member called me one night and asked for my help in removing some raccoons from a picnic shelter. A large function was to be held there the next day, and there was concern that two worlds would collide. After inspecting the structure, we finally found the young raccoon cubs lounging in the eaves of the shelter. The cubs were too young to accompany mom on her nightly forays, yet old enough to decide that we were up to no good, and once illuminated by a flashlight, they scattered throughout the confines of the rafter eaves. Since there was no trace of the mother around, and it was after dark, I guessed that she was out hunting and would return later to feed the cubs. I immediately suggested that since there was ample electricity available at the shelter, we could turn the night lights on and place a loud radio in the eaves. Most likely, when mom came back she would find those conditions unacceptable and immediately remove the young. But as it's been said, you can lead a horse to water...

My companions insisted that we could (and should) reach in with a catch pole and remove the cubs. Then they could be placed in a live trap as enticement for trapping the female. I had seen this scenario many times before. Some raccoons are easy to trap, but others—not so much. Not to mention, the time frame needed to get her into a trap even if she were so inclined. Fortunately, the cubs were adept at eluding us within the structure. (Okay, I admit I wasn't really trying that hard, but I was hoping no one would notice.)

Finally, we agreed to turn on all the lights. As luck would have it, a public address system was set up with the ability to pipe in music to the shelter. We selected a loud, obnoxious radio station and left for the evening.

I received a phone call the next day telling me that the raccoon family was indeed gone. Being of mature years, I resisted the urge to jump up and down yelling, *"Told ya so, told ya so!"* but instead graciously relayed my congratulations on the problem being solved in time for the picnic. Youth is indeed wasted on the young.

What we need to learn from these two examples is the concept, once again, of habitat modification. Loud and noisy versus dark and quiet. Risky and dangerous rather than safe and sound. Take away the main reasons that the animals are there in the first place, and they often decide to immediately leave on their own. These types of techniques can have limited effect in other situations, like with burrowing animals such as woodchucks or skunks. Their underground lairs are difficult to modify, and we often end up with the animal developing a bunker mentality and refusing to leave. Ammonia on a rag has often been suggested for skunks in a burrow, but I have no firsthand knowledge of its efficacy. It's worth trying though. Be sure to check the section on habitat modification for other tips and techniques.

A perceived nuisance wildlife scenario would be an animal or animals using the property but not necessarily causing any damage. This is usually made worse when the animal's presence has aroused someone's unreasonable fear. An example of this might be some variety of terrestrial mammals such as squirrels moving through, or temporarily foraging on the property. If the buildings are in good repair and not exploitable by squirrels, then there is no real problem. Once again, a little information and education can go a long way in changing someone's perception of the problem.

Wood chucks, or gophers, as they are sometimes called, often drive people nuts just by their presence. Although capable of raiding a garden here and there, most of the time a woodchuck just wants to graze in the grass and weeds, most often running for cover at the sight of people or pets. Sometimes I think it's the apparent impunity with which the large rodents waddle around the yard that ticks some people off. Maybe it has a burrow on the property, maybe not. They have an annoying habit of not recognizing property lines. Check for the presence of a burrow by looking for the main entrance marked by its tell-tale dirt mound. A hole with no mound is often a hidden back door to the burrow system. Then, ask yourself: Is this really a problem? Is there any actual damage? Do I really want to go to war over this one? Ironically, perceived nuisance problems rarely have a fix to them that will make everyone happy. With no actual damage to repair, cavity to exclude animals from, or with animals just moving through and using the area, it's tough to actually come up with a plan. That's because one often isn't needed other than a change of outlook by whoever's upset.

Trapping animals willy-nilly just creates voids in the habitat that nature will fill with another animal. Once again, it is habitat modification that has the only chance of providing any long-term benefits. Is the animal taking advantage of any cover that can be removed or modified? Are weeds cut down or bushes trimmed back? Is the animal getting under the fence somehow? Is this something that can be dealt with reasonably? Sometimes changing the path an animal must take can make things less attractive to them. Food, safety, and someplace to live are always foremost in a wild creature's mind, and therefore, must be foremost in ours if we are to be successful in abating potential nuisance problems.

Getting Professional Help

There are times when it may be necessary for the average person to enlist the services of a professional nuisance wildlife control operator, or NWCO. Most of these people are knowledgeable folks who are licensed, insured, and have the necessary equipment and expertise to handle the larger, difficult, or potentially dangerous nuisance wildlife scenarios that sometimes can occur. A large-scale bat infestation, for example, is a good time to involve a pro. Likewise is the handling and removing of certain large mammals that are trapped and not able to escape on their own. These are situations where getting qualified help is usually better for every-one— people and animals. There are, however, some points to consider when seeking professional help.

Like any service-oriented business you would consider for your home or property, are they insured? Licensed? Can they provide you with references?

What is their policy with regard to the disposition of any animals removed, and are you comfortable with that policy? Are they willing to transfer any orphaned animals to a wildlife rehabilita-tor? It might be a good idea to avoid any operators who attempt to scare you into hiring them with horror stories of disease and animal attack. Find out ahead of time if their services include the vital exclusion and repair work, along with any animal removal, to insure that the problem does not reoccur. Remember that many of these people are creditable professionals that are providing a necessary service and must be paid reasonably for doing it.

Many homeowners are angry and reluctant to pay for professional animal removal. Strangely, they often feel that because it's not their fault that the animal problem has occurred, they shouldn't have to pay for a solution. When I have occasion to speak with people regarding this attitude, I remind them that if the wind blows hard and tears some shingles off the roof, or if the furnace quits running in the middle of winter, they will need to have qualified people with the necessary skills come out and fix the problem. It is essentially the same thing. In reality, it is home repair of a different sort. Indeed, if it were a more common type of home repair, there would never be any discussion or reluctance at all. My favorite type of complaint here involves senior citizens. At the risk of getting hate mail, or death threats from AARP, let me pick on the older folks a minute. Just about every time it begins to look like professional help will be needed, the first thing out of their mouths is, "I can't afford a professional; I'm on a fixed income." Pardon me, but doesn't that include everyone but perhaps the independently wealthy? Excuse me folks, but I'm on a fixed income too, and as of this writing, I'm years away from retirement! My paycheck doesn't go up when things go wrong. Most of us manage to clothe and feed ourselves, and heat our homes come what may, in spite of what life throws at us. It is the same with some nuisance wildlife problems.

Chapter 5 - **Exotics**

The term exotic can be somewhat vague in describing animals, unless we are sure of the context. People often think of large reptiles, such as boa constrictors or pythons, generally as exotics. Or, there are a variety of small mammals considered exotics that are common to the pet trade. Sometimes it's just geography that defines it. For example, someone living in Maine might consider an alligator an exotic. Yet a person who resides in Florida sees it as a common part of the landscape. The moose is a large member of the deer family that is confined largely to subarctic wetlands and the extreme northeastern United States. Finding one in the middle of Kansas could label it an exotic. Although now widely captive-bred, many species of tropical snakes and lizards are, or were, common to their place of origin.

Really, I believe we need to think of exotics generally as wildlife from somewhere else!

One of the backlashes we are experiencing is the displacement and artificial establishment of non-native species in various places around the country. Florida and the surrounding Southeast are perfect examples of this problem. Over the past few years, Florida wildlife officials have removed a startling number of large constrictors from area wetlands. Large constrictors of tropical origin, such as the now common Burmese python and its subspecies, have been able to adapt to the warm, wet environment of southern Florida to the point where they can flourish and even breed. Nature has a system of delicate checks and balances. Often this system can tolerate inadvertent tinkering by man. But, sometimes it can't. Those familiar with the Everglades and surrounding wetlands of the region were aware of the distinct lack of 20-foot snakes, capable of killing and eating small and large mammals of all kinds, just a few years ago. No longer. This type of invasion into delicate ecosystems has wildlife biologists understandably concerned.

It's not just the big snakes. There are many species that have been introduced mostly through the misguided intentions of people releasing unwanted or uncared for exotic pets. A quick check through some Florida fish and game resources revealed this:

Florida's Exotic Wildlife: Status for 48 Reptile Species

Estimated trend in populations

- Seventeen species are expanding.

- Two species are stable.

- Four species are declining.

- Twenty-five species have unknown population levels.

Breeding status

- Thirty-five species have been breeding at least 10 years (but not necessarily consecutive years).

- Ten species are less than 10 years old.

- Three species are not reported breeding in the wild in Florida.

Established status

- Thirty-six established populations are confirmed breeding and apparently self-sustaining for 10 or more consecutive years.

- Two species are present and breeding but for less than 10 years.

- Eight species are present but not confirmed to be breeding. Population persists only with repeated introductions and/or escapes of individuals.

• Two species have populations whose status is unknown.

Many states, along with Florida, are currently dealing with artificially introduced species. It remains to be seen whether or not some native species can withstand the pressures resulting from predation and competition for food and nesting resources. This alarming new trend spells hardship or extinction for many species of indigenous plant and animal life throughout the country.

People who have an interest in keeping exotic animals must think long and hard about some important issues. First of all, what is it and why do I want to keep it? Also how will I keep an animal and what would the alternative be if I found myself not able to maintain it? The answers to these questions can have a profound impact not only on the quality of life for an individual animal but also perhaps on the very survival of entire ecosystems.

We are living in a world where, by virtue of our manipulation of information, technology, and wealth, we, in the United States, can have access to just about any type of exotic or nonnative animal we choose. However, we are left with the age-old axiom: because I can doesn't always mean I should.

Some may be thinking at this point that perhaps the subject of escaped or illegally held exotic animals may be a little overblown. Consider the fact that in a little over a decade of animal shelter medicine, animal rescue, and wildlife rehabilitation; I have personally dealt with the following exotic animals:

• Dozens of large constrictors including one in particular, commonly seen on a popular reality TV show (Bad boys, bad boys, whatchya gonna do?)

• A large timber wolf

- Several really large carnivorous lizards of Asian origin

- Many illegally imported American alligators

- A dozen or so South American caimans, including two found swimming in local recreational city parks

- An African monitor lizard found strolling through a nearby suburb

- A copperhead hiding in a box of flowers

- A timber rattlesnake

- More iguanas than I can count

- A South American anaconda

- A truckload (literally) of soft-shelled turtles

- Poison dart frogs

- Increasing numbers of sulcata tortoises (large burrowing tortoises) that were found at large, and burrowing

Many so-called exotic animals end up leading less than quality lives. Tropical animals have specific temperature and humidity requirements. Large carnivores can be dangerous to handle. Many people are not equipped to deal with the burden of providing the proper diets for many of these animals.

There are instances where some of these animals can be humanely kept by average people under average conditions, but many animals in the pet trade have a short life and a senseless death.

Chapter 6 - **Animal Entrapments**

One kind of entrapment scenario is lurking in many backyards today: the swimming pool. Topping the list of victims are ducklings. Swimming pools can also be a hazard for small mammals. Squirrels, moles, rabbits, and other various rodents can all blunder into the pool and end up in the skimmer. Most are too small to negotiate the lip of the pool and hopelessly swim around until they succumb to exhaustion. If you find this happening, get a mesh laundry bag and hang it over the edge in the pool when you're done swimming. Weight down the other end on the deck with something. This provides an escape ladder that many small creatures can easily climb out with.

There are other man-made traps that wildlife periodically falls into. One of the most common is the commercial dumpster. Here, the raccoon gets in trouble most of the time; dumpsters just smell too good to a raccoon. Outside design features and topography assist the raccoons in gaining entry, but the smooth inside walls of most commercial waste containers make it difficult or impossible to escape from.

At this point, let me be clear that most, if not all animal entrapments, are not really nuisance wildlife situations that need to end with an animal being removed from the area. This, once again, is habitat driven and things can usually be corrected or set right.

Barring any obvious signs of illness or injury to the animal, the easiest way to solve a dumpster or similar entrapment is to provide a means of escape for the trapped animal. One of the quickest ways is to slide a plank or two-by-four down into the dumpster at the shallowest angle possible and give the animal time to climb out on its own.

The animal doesn't always figure it out in 10 minutes, so checking on it every 10 minutes doesn't help. Give it a couple of hours if need be.

Window wells can be traps for smaller creatures like juvenile cottontails and skunks. The plank or ramp method can be used here too, along with wrapping an old towel around the plank to provide the animals with better footing. You can also try carefully lifting them out with a shovel. There are clear plastic window-well covers available that not only permanently prevent animals from falling in but also provide a solar advantage to the home in winter.

Trash cans seem to be a hazard for opossums. This one is simple. Just tip the can over and let them out. I'm constantly surprised at how reluctant people are to do this. Folks just don't want to let them go. Opossums are everywhere. And once again, if our property is secure, the animals will go on their way if given the opportunity.

There are certain types of fencing that can be a hazard for wildlife. Sometimes there is nothing that can really be done to prevent an entrapment. Wrought iron or simulated wrought iron fencing can fool deer into thinking they can squeeze through it. Deer are incapable of realizing that the fence will not give way like the brush they move through most of the time.

What occurs, then, is the deer attempts to run right through the fence and often gets trapped between the bars or literally impaled over top of it. This is a serious situation and not one I would recommend most people get directly involved with. White-tailed deer are incredibly powerful animals and are more than capable of seriously injuring someone.

In the event that a deer is trapped between the fence bars and is discovered relatively quickly, if a rope can be attached to each bar on either side of the deer, enough pulling force can sometimes be applied to spread the bars and free the deer without getting too close to it. Working on the back side of the fence is recommended so that if you are successful in freeing the animal, you now have the fence between you and the frightened deer.

Chain-link fencing can sometimes snare animals like rabbits and woodchucks that try to pass through the diamond shaped openings. Again this is driven by the animals' inability to discern the fence as an immovable object. Heavy-duty linesman's pliers or bolt cutters can sometimes cut through the fence wire and free the animal with minimal damage to the fence. If it appears that the animal has been entangled for a prolonged period of time, slide a trash can or other container around the animal and work from the opposite side of the fence. When freed, the animal will be automatically contained should it need medical assistance.

Another strange hazard is the shepherd hook used to hang plants in the yard. Right where the wrought iron starts its bend, typically there is an ornamental curl on the opposite side. The "Y" that forms there can be a trap for small birds. They evidently get a foot caught as they fly through the hook. Take a small piece of black electrical tape and place it over the "Y", eliminating the crevice.

One of my favorite backyard birds is the blue jay. Not everyone appreciates this bold, noisy little relative of the crow. Sporting a great paint job and a spunky attitude, this backyard visitor is common in many areas of the country. My mother appreciated them for their bold colors but held them in some contempt for their supposed bullying of other species. I had never witnessed any of this legendary behavior until recently.

I was rounding the corner of my garage one day when my eye caught the flash of a high-speed feathered pursuit that ended in a snow bank. Immediately, I assumed I had witnessed an attack by one of the smaller raptors common to my area. Perhaps, I thought to myself, an American kestrel or sharp-shinned hawk had chased down and apparently captured some other bird. To my surprise, a second later a blue jay emerged from the snow drift and after jumping to a low branch, smoothed its ruffled feathers and then was gone through the pine trees.

Curious to see who the vanquished was, I walked over to the spot and peered into the snow-covered clump of weeds at the edge of the yard. There lay a lifeless male cardinal, stone dead. I examined him for a moment as he lay in my hand. I found myself hoping perhaps he was just stunned, but he was indeed dead, his neck broken by the jay. He appeared fat, in good condition, and feather perfect. I must admit that for a moment I felt a little conflicted. As a wildlife rehabilitator, falconer, and long-time hunter, I am no stranger to death in the animal world. Indeed, I celebrate the cycle of give and take that is so vital to all life on earth. But the attack by the jay took me by surprise and up against my own standard of take what you need and use what you take—it was found wanting. Knowing nature would not let the cardinal's energy go to waste in this hard season, I laid the lifeless red bird on top of the snow drift and walked away to mull over what I'd just witnessed.

Animals are perfect creations in an imperfect world. They do what they have been designed to do, and there are reasons for their behavior even though they're not always readily apparent. After thinking it over, I assumed the jay's attack was born out of a need for food or territory. Although not an expert in corvid behavior, I do know that all life struggles for essentially the same things: food, water, and cover. In this respect, the jay was no different. The cardinal and the jay were occupying essentially the same niche together, so survival had forced the jay to kill the cardinal. I marveled once again at the intricacies of nature. A raptorial bird, such as a hawk or falcon, would have obviously converted the cardinal's energy in a more immediate fashion. The blue jay, on the other hand, had helped ensure its survival by eliminating the competition of the cardinal, thus making more energy available for itself in the long run. I'm sure that this happens far more often than we have any idea of.

It is my habit these days to take what nature teaches me and apply it somehow in my work. This often entails teaching others about how to live next door to wildlife. The conflict between the blue jay and the cardinal helps underscore a more common experience that troubles many backyard bird watchers. In practically every season of the year, I talk to people who are upset over songbird or small mammal predation by resident hawks, falcons, or owls. The names change but the complaint is usually the same: someone has one or more bird feeders and loves animals or is feeding wild birds because they will die otherwise. Then one day, one of the local birds of prey refuses to ignore the resource and finally makes a successful kill. No matter that the predator has most likely failed in 8 out of 10 attempts and, more often than not, is on the edge of starvation itself. It is the initial reaction of most people to assign some sort of blame to the carnivore. Out of this blame, and sometimes guilt, it is decided that the smaller birds or mammals must be "protected" from the evil predators. In other words, it's great to have wildlife around, until it starts behaving like wildlife, and then it's a different story!

It's easy to say I don't want any hawks killing my songbirds, but how about songbirds killing songbirds? Or red squirrels that do not often tolerate the larger gray squirrels when habitats get small. The adorable chipmunk is one of the chief predators of songbird nests. Crows will never pass up the opportunity to torment any bird of prey, and just about all birds of prey will attack and feed on each other. It's a jungle out there folks, so where exactly do we draw the line at trying to control what occurs in our backyard?

Opossums are amazing creatures and North America's only marsupial. Though historically maligned for everything from raiding chicken houses to spreading disease, they are in fact immensely beneficial to the environment. And, being omnivorous, they are not above cleaning up under the bird feeder when things get a little messy. Most of the time when they are caught performing these janitorial duties, the reaction from most people can be somewhat negative. Not everyone thinks opossums are cute (as for me I still haven't decided). Personally though, I would much rather have an opossum clean up a potential food source and then leave, as this nomadic animal always does, rather than have a potential rat or mouse problem later on. Opossums move around a lot, while rats and mice usually come to stay, not to mention the fact that opossums will feed on mice if given the opportunity.

Squirrels raiding bird feeders really tick some people off. My advice is simple here: either build or invest in the best squirrel-proof technology you can afford, and then get used to the idea that sooner or later some squirrel will figure out how to beat it. That's their job! Don't like it? Don't feed. Trying to remove the squirrels just makes more room for more squirrels.

As humans, we are adept at manipulating our environment. However, we don't always think things through. The feeding of songbirds and other forms of wildlife can be a fun, fascinating, and educational pastime and can arguably provide a supplemental source of food for a limited number of local animals in your area. But along with the artificial attraction and concentration of wildlife that can occur with a feeding program, we sometimes get some things that we did not bargain for. When that happens, we need to try and understand things from the animals' point of view. Although most of us feed birds and other wildlife for our own enjoyment, we would do well to remember that it is not always about us.

The connections that exist between people and animals are complex and sometimes difficult to explain. People can get really emotional when it comes to animals. This can be a really good thing or a really bad thing. Most of the time when people try to navigate wildlife issues strictly by emotion, they end up making things much worse than if they had done nothing at all.

Emotions can cloud good judgment, create bad decisions, stand in the way of education, and even cause injury to animals and humans alike.

Fear and anger are some of the most common emotions expressed when the human and animal worlds collide. However, I have found that these two emotions, though volatile, are easy to help people through with a little patience. Once I begin to educate people about the animals they are dealing with, fear and anger begin to subside. Guilt is another powerful force in animal situations. People feel bad at the thought of something negative happening to an animal. Nuisance wildlife scenarios are a good example of this. In the course of educating someone, absolving them of any guilt can make all the difference.

More often than not, when people are confronted with wildlife, their first thoughts go something like this: Will this animal attack me? Is my family in danger? In reality, under normal circumstances wild animals have no interest in getting mixed up with people. No kidding, it is the last thing on their minds! Understand that what I mean by normal circumstances might be an animal on the property or in the backyard, or one living in the attic, shed, barn or outbuilding. These animals are merely moving through their environment, sometimes taking advantage of spaces or resources we unwittingly provide for them.

Different species have developed different levels of tolerance and adaptations to the way we live. For example, the Cooper's hawk is a fairly common, though rarely noticed, urban resident. Historically, these birds were always considered forest dwellers by nature, using cover to ambush their prey, which consists mostly of various small birds. These days, it is arguable that more of these diminutive hawks can be found in the cities and suburbs where songbirds and pigeons abound in parks, golf courses, and backyard bird feeders. Although adapted to city life, they have little tolerance for humans and so, rarely linger where they can be easily viewed at length.

In contrast, Canada geese can be seen just about anywhere and in exactly the same habitat. Incredibly tolerant of people, geese are happy to go about their business within a few feet of human activity of all kinds. Obviously, both Cooper's hawks and Canada geese are birds, but they differ in their habits and the way they live their lives next to us. Like most wildlife we may encounter from time to time, both of these birds have the ability to defend themselves when necessary. Larger mammals like raccoons and foxes, because of their sometimes formidable appearance, tend to make people very uneasy when they turn up close to humans. Although both of these species are very observant and comfortable living close to us, most people assume that there must be something wrong with the animals when they encounter them. The fact is these and other mammals are very observant of the world around them; they have to be in order to survive. This behavior allows them to become very familiar with our routines and daily movements. It is really just an application of their natural behavior.

Birds of prey have fascinated man since the beginning of recorded history. There are many species of hawks, falcons, eagles, and owls that can be viewed all over North America, either as temporary migrants or permanent residents. A few of the most common are the Cooper's hawk that I mentioned before, the red-tailed hawk, the diminutive American kestrel, the screech owl, and the great horned owl. These five interesting birds are some of the most likely to be encountered in and around our cities and suburbs. To people unfamiliar with these unique animals, one of the most common misconceptions is that children and pets are at risk when some of the larger species are found nearby. Even a young red-tailed hawk is an impressive sight soaring over our homes or perched on a utility pole. It is easy to see how myth and imagination have them carrying off our favorite pet. In reality, that same red-tailed hawk is much better suited to feeding on small mammals, most of them being the size of mice and rats. A large prey animal for a bird the size of the red-tailed hawk might be a cottontail rabbit.

Birds of prey of all species are keenly aware of what their natural food looks like and how it behaves, and what their own physical limitations are. We need to remember that, as with all wildlife, they mean us no harm. All animals have instincts that help them survive. We as a species have few survival instincts, but instead rely on thought and common sense. Animals instinctively know that aggression that leads to fighting can cost them their lives, and so, most will avoid it at all costs. It is one reason why many species are capable of such elaborate body language. Any animal that becomes cornered or trapped, on purpose or through circumstance, will do what it thinks it must do to survive. How we respond in these instances sometimes makes all the difference.

When things get really tough, what I call "severe, uncontrollable hand wringing" begins. One example of this is when young species

49

of mammals are found. Those of us that work with wildlife know that, more often than not, young animals are not orphaned but merely waiting for the next period of contact with the adults: nursing, brooding, etc. It is rare for an adult animal of any species to spend a great deal of time with newborn young until they are strong enough and old enough to emerge from a den and travel with the adults. This holds true for rabbits, deer, squirrels, and birds of all kinds. I have spent a great deal of time over the years trying to make some people understand things like female cottontails are rarely seen near the nest, or that white-tailed deer stash their fawns for several days after birth, only returning to nurse them and often to move their location.

Even though people can intellectually grasp what they're being told, many can't bring themselves to leave well enough alone. This challenge, though emotionally based, more often than not has its roots in simple ignorance such as a lack of knowledge of the basic biology and habits of the animal in question.

Yet another popular attitude is that because the animal lives near people, and/or people have been feeding it, it is now somehow incapable of surviving without some sort of human intervention. Wildlife, rarely if ever, needs our help to survive. Animals are complete in form and function, and most of the time, with the exception of perhaps feeding songbirds; we usually end up making things more difficult for wild animals by feeding them. Deer, for example, will quickly learn to show up regularly if food is put out for them. They will quickly disappear when the feeding stops. If they are seen in the area, it is usually because some other natural food source exists. The deer that takes advantage of artificial feeding is in no way incapable of foraging on its own. This is true of most wild creatures.

All habitats have an inherent carrying capacity limited by the amount of food and cover, and this provides much of the governing force behind which animals live and which die. Good-natured meddling does little at best and, at its worst, can make things much tougher for wildlife. It's true that many wild animals do not survive, and some can lead startlingly short lives under the best of circumstances. While at first glance cruel, this is just part of an awesome and perfect design that governs not only the wildlife in our neighborhood but all life on Earth.

Is there a time when it is appropriate to help? Are there any rules? The answer to both questions is yes!

Wildlife is under constant pressure these days, mostly from loss of habitat, but also from things like pollution, automobiles, power lines, etc. These types of things, while they do not always take away habitat, sometimes change the face of it to the point of setting up hazards or obstacles that often negatively impact wildlife. Natural predation and population dynamics aside, a songbird striking a window, birds of prey getting electrocuted on power poles, and countless mammals being hit along the highway are senseless and sad ways to lose a valuable resource. Can we stop these types of occurrences? Probably not.

Those without proper training and equipment must never attempt to handle, pet, or pick up injured wildlife. This is different from the simple non-invasive methods of confining an injured animal with a cardboard box or laundry basket. This, more often than not, is the only interaction necessary when encountering injured wildlife. If the animal proves confinable through simple means, then it is probably sick or injured to the point where aid by a qualified and licensed wildlife rehabilitator may help. If the animal is able to elude us, there is most likely nothing we could do to help it anyway. Your local office of fish and game or department of natural resources usually has a list or a way for you to contact a wildlife rehabilitator in your area. They may be able to come and get the animal and render the appropriate aid. Try and consult with them before doing anything. In general, it is never a good idea to feed any injured animal that we may temporarily have in our possession. Oddly, it is the most common mistake humans make when confronted with wildlife. I call it "the chicken soup mentality."

Somehow, we as a species think that whatever is wrong with the animal can be fixed with food. And yet intellectually, most of us are aware that if we were in an accident, the paramedics would not be rushing us off to the nearest McDonald's!

Wild creatures live a totally different existence than we do. It just so happens they sometimes live it right on our doorstep. If it were up to the animals, they would choose to live their lives going unnoticed among us. If we are able to help an injured animal appropriately, this can be considered, at the very least, good conservation and respect for our natural resources.

Wildlife Rehabilitators

Less than 30 years ago, wildlife rehabilitation, the art and science of treating injured wildlife, was pretty much in its infancy with no real organization and very little science. In a few short years there has been much change. There are now many state-level wildlife councils, state permitting systems, and seminars at the state, national, and local levels. Also there is more and more networking between rehabilitators all the time. The art has gone from mere guesswork to targeted diets, approved techniques, accepted minimum standards for housing and handling, etc. Some rehabilitators specialize in one or more species, while others care for any creature in trouble.

Wildlife rehabilitators are very dedicated people who, for the most part, always have the animal's best interest at heart. They can be a valuable resource for anyone with potential wildlife-related problems, questions, or encounters with sick and injured wildlife. Your local department of natural resources, or DNR office or state game officials can often put you in touch with local wildlife rehabilitators in your area. Anyone encountering wildlife that they think is in trouble and needs assistance would do well to contact a local rehabilitator first before deciding on a course of action with an animal.

With any art or science, much opinion exists with regards to how it should be practiced. Wildlife rehabilitation also sparks controversy when the question is broached: should we?

It is no secret that wild animals can lead very short lives. Life on earth is tough, and in many respects, it's getting tougher all the time. One may ask, what is the point? After all, it is not nature's intent for all animals to survive, so why invest the material and emotional resources into something that we seemingly have no control over? I believe there are several reasons that almost have to change with the species.

For example, there is more than enough anecdotal evidence to support the success of rehabilitating certain avian species such as raptors. There have been many instances when banded hawks have turned up again, sometimes several decades later. Indeed, once these birds get past the critical first year or two, their survivability goes up exponentially. So their resiliency is unquestionable. It is easier to make a case for treating and releasing an adult breeding member of a population such as a red-tailed hawk, for example. Particularly when such an animal performs such a needed role in the environment: controlling rodent populations, etc. When the discussion turns to other smaller and more biologically numerous animals that exist farther down the food chain, we often need to look a little further.

I often refer to cottontail rabbits as being one notch above grass in the food chain. This may seem harsh to some. Don't get me wrong; I like rabbits. I admire their resiliency and their ability to survive conditions that we would never consider going out the door in. But I also know that with their average life span being around 9 months, and the fact that cottontails actively reproduce up to 7 months out of the year, it is clear to me what much of their job is, and that is feeding other animals.

That being said, personally I view the rehabilitation and release of these amazing little creatures as akin to planting grass or trees. They are part of the substance of which a food web is built on. A wise man builds his house upon a rock, and you cannot have other more complex forms of life without a solid foundation underneath them. It is simply good stewardship to engage in the raising and releasing of these creatures. Those of us that plant trees and grasses know that not all that we plant survives. Yet we know it is the right thing to do.

I have a special admiration for predators. I sometimes feel for them like most people feel for the fuzzier or "cuter" forms of wildlife. I know they have a much harsher life at times than say, an obligate herbivore like a rabbit or deer. Their very existence depends on their ability to locate prey and hunt it successfully.

They don't get to stand around and graze, or spend dormant periods waiting for things to improve. They have to make something happen or go hungry. It almost makes me want to complain less about getting up in the morning for work. (I said almost.) The rehabilitation of these important animals is just as vital, if not more so. From insects, to rodents, to rabbits and deer, predators help keep animal populations healthy. There are instances when predator numbers can conceivably get high, but it is far from the norm. The predator-prey relationship is a self-limiting one, and if an opportunity exists to place an animal back into the environment to do the job it was created to do, then we must take it.

Losing our valuable resource of wildlife to some dumb senseless demise, such as an automobile collision, pollution, high tension wire, or uncontrolled development, is a sad thing. Doing nothing when there are options available is even sadder.

Blue Jay with Newly Hatched Chicks

During the spring and summer months, it's common for people (and pets) to find the nests and dens of baby birds and mammals. Human nature compels people to assume that the babies are abandoned because often there are no parent animals in sight. It is at this point that people remove the babies from the nest or den, thinking that the babies are orphaned. Fledgling birds, young cottontail rabbits, and fawns are common victims of this scenario. In reality, most wild animal parents have specific behavior patterns that help protect their young from danger. This often includes avoiding the nest or den location so as not to reveal the location to potential predators. A person should only attempt a rescue if the young appear limp, cold, lethargic, or lifeless. If you are unsure whether an animal is orphaned or not, contact a local wildlife rehabilitator for advice. Let's take a look at some common wildlife in our backyards, and how we should respond to finding the young of some species.

Baby Rabbits

The eastern cottontail is a common urban resident. Nests of rabbits are typically discovered by gardening activities or curious pets in the backyard. Baby rabbits that have smooth, slick fur and ears lying back should be left in the nest. Small, with eyes closed, and helpless, these tiny young cause concern in people when discovered. Even though not readily seen, the mother rabbit is usually there and on the job, feeding them at the nest, under cover of darkness. I advise people to leave the nest alone, keep the family dog away, and most of the time, in a very few weeks, the young are on their own. There is no need to be concerned about the old myth that once the babies have been touched, the mother will not nurse them. A great way to monitor a nest to be sure mom is on the job is to lay string, dental floss, or lightweight sticks across the nest in a grid-like pattern extending about 2 inches past the perimeter of the nest. Check back after the next dark cycle to see if the mother returned under cover of darkness to feed the young.

If a nest is discovered in the lawn, the good news is cottontails grow very quickly. From birth until emergence from the nest is a process that only takes between 3 ½ to 4 weeks. If the family dog is too curious, take a cardboard box big enough to cover the nest, and then tip it upside down over it and cut a doghouse door in one side. Make it big enough for the female rabbit to crawl in and nurse the young. Weigh the box down with a small rock or some sticks and let the rabbits do the rest. If there is a worry about a lawn mower mishap, marking the boundary of the nest with sticks will usually suffice.

Cottontail rabbits grow amazingly fast. Often people mistake small emergent cottontails as orphaned when they are, in fact, ready to be on their own. In part, this is because newly emerged cottontails have no other defense but to freeze in the presence of danger. They have not yet perfected the ability to flee rapidly from a threat. Another reason many people mistakenly think the young rabbits are orphaned is the fact that most of the time we see only the adults out in the open. Juvenile rabbits often stay under cover until they are stronger and faster.

Remember, not seeing the mother close by or not seeing her at all, is normal. Hamster-size rabbits with their ears up and spiky-looking fur are old enough to be on their own and should be returned to the tall grass. One of the concerns for many people returning young cottontails to the wild is the presence of cats. A natural reaction for many people is immediate concern regarding the risk to the rabbits. We need to keep in mind that there are cats everywhere, along with a number of other more natural predators that the rabbits must deal with. Our desire to relocate the young in these instances is not warranted, nor practical. However, because of the high risk of infection, any young cotton-tails that have confirmed contact with cats (or any other pets), whether bitten or merely picked up by them, should most likely be seen by a wildlife rehabilitator for treatment.

Baby Squirrels

Springtime means windy weather and seasonal tree trimming. This can cause trouble sometimes for nesting gray squirrels. Babies blown from the nest or inadvertently evicted during tree cutting or cleanup is a very common occurrence. Often times when given the opportunity, female squirrels will move the babies to a safe location. Delaying the completion of a tree cutting or trimming job once a nest is discovered and giving the mother time to move the exposed young is often the best way to keep them from being orphaned.

Squirrels are quite prolific, usually giving birth to litters twice each year. Baby squirrels are born in early spring and in late summer. Many squirrels build their nests from woven leaves high in the trees. In contrast to cottontail rabbits, baby squirrels mature much more slowly. It is a process that, in the wild, lasts months rather than weeks. During this time, baby squirrels stay in the nest. They make their home in the nest until fully weaned at about 3 months of age.

In the event that something happens to the mother squirrel, and if the babies are old enough to react to their hunger, they will come out and often will end up on the ground. If the female is able, she will come down and return the young squirrels to the nest. Baby squirrels found on the ground should be placed in a shallow container or box and left at the base of the tree for as long as possible to allow the mother the opportunity to retrieve them. During cooler weather, a plastic soda bottle filled with hot water and wrapped in a towel can be placed in the container with the babies to help keep them warm while waiting for the female to arrive. Remember to give the mother squirrel some space so as not to frighten her. Any squeaking or other vocalizations by the young should only encourage the mother to rescue them.

Baby Birds

The call on the phone is all too familiar. *"We have this bird here... We think it may be injured..."*

Mid-spring through summer is fledgling season. This can be a season that many wildlife rehabilitators dread. While most people think that baby birds grow up in the nest and then fly away, nature has a different idea. In reality, most birds grow in the nest up to a certain stage and then fledge, or leave the nest and fly to the ground. As fledglings, the young birds are still cared for on the ground by the adults for a number of days while they develop the necessary skill and strength for flight. With many species, such as crows and robins, the young birds are nearly as large as the adult birds that are caring for them. This scenario, in one form or another, is common throughout the bird world.

Many people come across fledgling birds in their yards from early May right through the summer. These birds are commonly thought to be injured in some way because of their poor flying abilities. It is very common for these young birds to be found just about anywhere on the ground, often sitting in one place for long periods of time waiting for the adult birds to bring them food. Fledglings can often be easily identified by their short tail feathers and slightly fuzzy appearance around the head.

The all too common statement I encounter from the public after explaining the behavior of fledgling birds is, *"But you don't under-stand...We have cats in our neighborhood!"* The reality is most of us who work with wildlife understand all too well how cats fit into the picture.

Many centuries ago we took the cat out of the wild, but in some ways we have yet to take the wild out of the cat. In short, the common cat, Felis domesticus, will always be a predator to some degree. It is the intersection of the predatory instincts of the cat and the ground-dwelling nature of young birds that causes an annual conflict.

Depending on local cat populations, time of year, and human involvement, cats can prey on significant numbers of birds and other wildlife in certain locales. A few objective studies have been done on a large scale, but results are not clear as to the overall impact on individual species. However, many birds and small mammals are brought to wildlife rehabilitators each year suffering from injuries resulting from cat attacks.

The initial reaction from the public regarding cats threatening wildlife is the belief that the problem can be simply remedied by someone coming out and "relocating" or "rescuing" the bird. The reality is that if it were actually possible to assist the staggering number of birds or animals in this situation, it would be a largely unrewarding task for a number of reasons.

First of all, cats are everywhere these days. Whether in the country or the city, cats are a fact of life for wildlife. There really is no place that someone can "relocate" a young bird to and guarantee its absolute safety.

It is also not in the fledgling's best interest to deprive it of the valuable interaction it has with the adult birds. It is possible and sometimes appropriate for qualified, licensed individuals to rescue and raise legitimately orphaned wildlife, but the hard truth is nobody raises a wild animal better than its parents.

Another aspect to the fledgling problem is that there are many natural predators of young birds other than cats. Hawks, raccoons, skunks, and foxes are all animals that prey, at one time or another, on birds, but it is the cats that are readily seen and recognized by most people and thus perceived to be the only challenge for the young birds. A fledgling on the ground in the process of mastering its flight skills has much to cope with and many dangers to avoid if it is to be successful. The best way we can help is to leave fledgling birds alone (unless we are certain they are injured) and to keep our cats indoors.

The bat is, oddly enough, generally considered to be one of the most feared animals in the world. There is some kind of visceral reaction that takes place with most of us when we find ourselves face to face with one of these tiny, harmless, winged mammals. It will most likely drive many to distraction when they learn that most buildings harbor at least a couple of bats. They are everywhere and quite common in city, suburb, and country environs. Most of the time bats are exploiting cavities that are associated with a particular building's architecture and that have little or nothing to do with human living space. Bats can take advantage of cracks, holes, and crevices that exist in just about every structure, old or new.

One of the most important things to remember when dealing with bats is the nickel rule, meaning that any crack, hole, crevice, or separation in a structure that has a surface area the size of a nickel will generally provide enough space for a bat to crawl in. Bats can live in the eaves, soffits, fascia, and attic spaces of our homes for years, never being detected, let alone becoming a real nuisance problem. At dusk they crawl out of whatever hole they are roosting in and spend the evening hunting insects with the aid of their natural echo-location abilities. They are usually back in the roost before full daylight.

This natural and beneficial process goes awry when, for whatever reason, the bat finds itself within the living space of the home or building. All of a sudden things get exciting. Children wail. Women shriek. Grown men cry. Someone's telephone begins to ring. The bat has already decided by now it has made a mistake and just wants out. That's all it wants. Just out. Bats don't want to attack us. Or suck our blood. Or even lay their eggs in our hair. (That would be a good trick for any mammal.) For some perverted reason known only to God and the bats, they are not nearly as good at finding their way out as they are at finding their way in. Echo-locate a sand fly and catch it on the wing in the dark? No problem. Find the stupid hole they crawled through into your bedroom at midnight? No way. So what now? First the tough part—everybody calm down.

Imagine trying to echo-locate your way out of unfamiliar territory with large potential predators making lots of noise and running around while you're orbiting the room trying to figure out what went wrong. Sure, it looks easy. You try it. The first thing for us to do is to try and use the terrain at hand to our advantage. If the bat is in a room with a door, let's close it. Now at least all the hysteria is confined to one room. Is there a window in the room? Let's open it. Most of the time, the bat will gravitate toward the window once it begins to differentiate the open space from all the echoes it has been getting back off the walls. Try to stay in the room and be still for a couple minutes, so draw straws if you have to, to see who gets to stay. Then you can easily verify that the bat did indeed escape. This can often prevent you from suddenly sleeping alone if you didn't go to bed that way in the first place.

If you have the bat confined in a room with no window, there are still some options at this point. You want to avoid touching the bat with your bare hands. I realize this is the farthest thing from most of our minds, but I feel the need to say it anyway. In most areas, bats are classified as a rabies vector species. It doesn't mean your bat has rabies, it just means that bats are known to sometimes carry the virus. It is not a reason to panic as much as an opportunity for some common sense. In the event that some-one is bitten, it often amounts to more paperwork and possibly some post-exposure rabies vaccinations. To prevent this, simply donning a pair of gloves of just about any type will provide the necessary protection. Often, after flying around and bumping into the walls, the bat will begin to tire. Be prepared with an old towel or T-shirt. When the bat alights on the floor, simply toss the towel over it. Then gently scoop it up in the towel and take it outside. Gently release him in the shrubbery or grass, and the bat, once getting its bearings, will be off without a word of thanks. Before you do this, call your local county health department to make sure they do not, for some reason, want to examine the bat. Different municipalities have different protocols when it comes to species that have a higher instance of carrying the rabies virus. If the bat comes up missing and you're fairly certain it did not escape outside, look for it roosting behind standing or hanging pictures on the wall, doors, toilets, closets, between hanging clothing, in shoes, behind dressers, etc. Find the places where you initially would think that it would be impossible for the bat to be and look there first.

A roosting bat that has gone dormant and is hanging on the wall, picture frame, etc., can be easily captured by placing a 1-pound coffee can or equivalent over it, and sliding a piece of cardboard or paper under it, trapping the bat in the can. Many people refuse to do this and insist on calling a professional nuisance wildlife removal agent to come to the home at great expense to remove the offending creature. This is certainly a viable option, and there are many qualified people willing to come and provide this service. The method they usually employ to remove the bat is as follows: They place a 1-pound coffee can or its equivalent over the bat and slide a piece of paper or cardboard under it, trapping the bat in the can. Then they hand you a bill.

Over time, older homes can accumulate cracks and crevices leading into the interior living spaces, allowing bats to migrate through, searching for food or responding to warmer or cooler temperatures. Hot summer weather or a sudden cold snap can often trigger this type of activity.

There are times when bats can cause actual unhealthy infestations. This usually occurs when they are allowed to roost in areas where people and domestic pets can come into contact with bat droppings. When infestations are suspected, it is prudent to get a thorough home inspection by a qualified nuisance control operator, preferably one who is experienced with bat problems. Solving this type of problem entails the same components as any other nuisance wildlife situation. Removal or eviction of the animals and the necessary exclusion work to prevent reentry. Because of the numbers involved in bat removal, the contractor often installs exclusion devices, which are essentially a one-way door that allows the bat to exit at will but not to reenter at the same point. Some of these devices are connected to a containment enclosure, while others just vent the bats to the outside of the structure and prevent their reentry.

Heavily used holes and roosting areas can often be identified by the staining that appears around the entrance. Often times, bats will land near a hole and crawl for several inches into the hole. Over time, oils from the bats' fur build up and can cause staining. This is a good way to identify a major roosting area. At the same time, the contractor will often begin to identify any other holes or cracks that might be used by bats and will fill them with various products depending on their size. These two methods, used concurrently, are standard practice for removing large numbers of bats.

Additional techniques, such as polyethylene sheeting, may have to be used in the home depending on the living space being affected. Poly sheeting is sometimes stapled to exposed rafters in attic spaces where there are large amounts of bat droppings. This, in effect, provides a barrier between any bat droppings and the living space, reducing or eliminating exposure.

Remedying large bat infestations, as well as finding someone to do the work, can be expensive and time consuming. Therefore, it is important to decide if an actual public health-related problem exists. As stated before, most structures, old and new, can harbor a few bats. Honest answers must be found first. Is this truly a public health issue, or is it a case of someone not wanting to come to grips with the fact that a few bats exist?

Most species of bats form maternity colonies in which to breed and raise their young. It is often these colonies that are involved in infestation scenarios. This is a summertime behavior that is opposite from the one or two bats found other times of the year, often during the winter when the weather warms temporarily.

There are several different species of bats that inhabit North America. Regardless of species, most bats generally have similar habits and can be dealt with in much the same way.

Chapter 12 - **Leave It To Beavers**

Beavers are large aquatic mammals that chew and feed on deciduous trees, often felling small trees in the process. They also make dams that can cause extensive flooding, sometimes resulting in damage to real estate and crops. Beavers can live in rivers, lakes, or streams—anywhere there is an adequate flow of water for damming. Beavers either build lodges to live in or live in burrows dug into the bank of a stream or river.

Beavers feed mainly on aquatic vegetation in warm weather and switch to woody browse in the winter. They are extremely active animals, constantly trying to build larger and larger dams, which can increase flooding. This behavior makes it easier for the beaver to move around in its aquatic environment, where it is constantly cutting tree branches and floating them off to pre-determined food caches.

Beavers are identified by their characteristic flat, paddle-like tails and webbed feet. They are much larger than most people think; beavers regularly achieve weights of up to 40 pounds or more.

Beaver control is usually better left to professionals. Removal, when warranted, often requires specially designed traps. Beavers' size and strength make trying to get them into conventional live traps a futile effort.

Trees can be protected from beavers by wrapping the trunks in metal mesh, or hardware cloth, to a distance of 15 inches above ground. Flooding by beavers can often be controlled by leaving the beavers in place and constructing an overflow device in the dam out of some form of culvert. In general, a 10- to 40- foot piece of culvert is positioned within the dam at the maximum water level desired.

A triangular, pointed weed guard is affixed to the upstream end of the culvert, which prevents beavers from blocking the flow. An alternate method is to install a 90-degree elbow that points straight up in the upstream end of the culvert, coinciding with the maximum water level. This usually makes it impossible for the beavers to block the vertical drain created. Removing food trees and raw building material from the shoreline can encourage beavers to move. Beavers cannot haul large amounts of material over dry land.

Trapping, removing, and relocating beavers is often highly re-stricted and controlled by state wildlife agencies, which usually require some sort of permit.

Red Tail Hawk

Birds of Prey

Autumn 1973

My first close encounter with a hawk was while out rabbit hunting one day. I was skulking through a grove of saplings that had a large dead tree at its center. I don't know what made me look up, but when I did, a mere 20 feet above me sat a large red-tailed hawk. The bird never moved but just stared down at me with that enigmatic yet disapproving look that they are all so capable of. As a young lad, I knew nothing of hawks except for the myth and bad PR passed on to me by my elders. Many years later I was to learn the truth about these amazing birds, and it would change my life. That day, however, I backed out of the thicket without taking my eyes off the bird. What I thought it was going to do to me, I have no clue. Thirty odd years ago they were nowhere near as common as they are today, and coming across one back then was sort of a big deal. I was 15 at the time, and I hadn't planned on seeing one of these birds that up close and personal. It startled me a little.

Bird of Prey Myths

I routinely talk to many people who have concerns about hawks on or around their property. Myth and legend have hawks, owls, and even eagles performing feats of strength and depredation far beyond their capacity or inclination. Usually the concern for most folks revolves around children and pets. Most concerns have to do with the several species of hawks and owls common to suburbia these days.

To the untrained observer, virtually all raptors look much bigger in flight than they really are. This fact alone is often the main reason we are left with accounts of birds of fantastic proportions, as much as 2 or 3 feet high with enormous wingspans. While it is true that the great horned owl, one of the largest owls in North America, has the ability to carry off some of the larger prey items on its menu, and the golden and bald eagles have enormous strength for their size, it is important to remember a couple of things. All birds of prey acquire through experience what are called search images, or in other words, what looks like prey to them. This is nearly without fail tempered with the innate knowledge that if they were to make a mistake and bind to something that could hurt them, such as a cat or dog, it could prove fatal to the bird. In addition, cats, dogs, and kids, no matter how small, do not move about or behave like prey and so, do not conform at all to the search image.

Let's take into account just one species of raptor, the red-tailed hawk, for example. This hawk is without question the most common bird of prey in the lower 48 states. They are literally everywhere. They inhabit every major ecosystem in North America. From deserts to coastal plains, and from sub arctic regions to the equator, we can sooner or later find a red-tailed hawk either soaring or sitting. Common sense alone tells us that if these birds were a threat to people and pets, the media (who always loves a good story) would be sounding the alarm almost daily. We would be reading weekly in the newspaper of the latest "attack" by some bird of prey. All that being said, the remains of feral cats have occasionally been discovered in the pellets of great horned owls. And, it is physically possible for, say, an unattended kitten to fall prey to a large raptor. We must remember these are instances that fall somewhat out of the norm. All birds of prey are uniquely created to hunt only those prey animals that are natural for them to pursue.

Winter 2005

My hunting partner and I split up and entered the thicket from both sides, both of us alert and watchful. We had hunted here before, and both of us fully expected to see some game with high odds for success.

As if on cue, a rabbit sprang from a snow-covered clump of grass at the base of a hawthorn and headed toward my partner. I yelled my usual warning, but it wasn't necessary. She had seen the rabbit too. Bandit, a large female red-tailed hawk, instantly leapt from her perch high in a poplar and was closing the distance to the cottontail that was streaking through the cover. I soon lost sight of the brown blur as it sped through the brush. My gaze shifted to the only remaining visi-

ble evidence of the drama unfolding before me—the hawk some 40 feet above in hot pursuit.

Depending on how one measures time and history, falconry, the ancient art of hunting with trained birds of prey, has been around for about 4,000 years. It has been said that man rode out of the mists of pre-history astride a horse, with a bird of prey on his fist, and a dog running out in front. It is with these three types of animals that man has had enduring relationships: relationships in which both man and animal have experienced mutual benefit. Horses and other beasts of burden have a natural behavior that has allowed their domestication. The dog willingly seeks our companionship out of its own social nature, and our relationship with it is quite remarkable. The bird of prey, through falconry, has learned to benefit by cooperatively hunting with people and yet can remain wild. Except in the case of cats, just about everything else we do amounts to merely keeping animals with no tangible benefits for either.

Somehow, somewhere, a man once fed a hawk. And when he did, the hawk remembered. In that moment of time long ago, falconry was born. Practiced throughout the ages and represented in many countries, falconry has a rich and varied history that can be traced back before the third century. Most of the works written down through the ages refer to falconry as practiced by kings, emperors, and other nobility. This is because the majority of the writings of the day were about those types of people, who also happened to be avid falconers. There is, however, significant evidence of lower and middle class involvement in the art throughout history.

Historic books on falconry are represented by such works as the 15th century Book of St. Albans, which lists the types of birds that could be used and by whom. Another famous tome, and one that is still relevant even by today's standards, is the 13th century De Arte Venandi cum Avibus (The Art of Falconry) by Emperor Frederick II of Hohenstaufen. Today there are a variety of modern books written on the subject of falconry. Although still practiced in much the same way as in ancient times, falconry has benefited tremendously from advances in science, animal health, medicine, and other technologies.

It is not clear how falconry came to North America, and how it compared to the sport in Europe and Asia; its tenure here is relatively new. One of the first falconry organizations in the United States is the Pennsylvania Peregrine Club, which can trace its roots back to 1933. In New York, there are dated photographs showing evidence of active falconry during the late 1930s and 1940s.

The cottontail did everything nature programmed it to do, to elude the hawk. It dodged left, then right. It dove in and out of the 6 inches of fresh, powdered snow and squirted through the thick vegetation. It would stop-and-go suddenly, hoping the hawk might fly over it. Finally, it entered a clump of brush and briar, where it apparently thought it would be safe. All this was made clear to me by watching my winged partner's flight across the field.

As I watched her, I thought of a recent conversation I had with some other falconers. The talk had turned to what kinds of birds we were flying. Upon hearing that I was flying a red-tail, one falconer, who had many years' experience, wistfully said, "Red-tails...they give you their heart and soul..." I knew exactly what he meant.

Suddenly the hawk pitched upwards into a short stall. With her forward motion halted, she began flapping her powerful wings to hold her position. I could see her looking straight down into the thicket beneath her...

I often wonder what she must think of me when we venture afield together. By now I have proven myself a worthy partner to her, assisting in the search for game and helping to assure her safety with potentially dangerous quarry such as a large gray squirrel or cock pheasant. But I wonder at times if she pities me for not being able to fly. We see birds every day, yet do we really appreciate what it is they do? It often gives me pause as I watch her spread her wings and step into space as casually as you or I would walk across a room.

In the blink of an eye, she rolled over sharply into a near vertical dive, pulling her wings in to become a brush-penetrating missile. I stood and watched in awe as the bird crashed into the seemingly impenetrable cover of thorn and vine in an attempt to catch her prey.

Falconry in North America is one of the most highly regulated forms of hunting. In addition to obtaining federal and state permits, hunters must pass a written exam and enter into a 2-year apprenticeship under the guidance of a general or master class falconer.

Although defined as hunting, falconry has also been referred to as a highly evolved form of bird watching. It hinges on the cooperation between a trained bird of prey and a dedicated human. The art requires much from the human member of the team. Knowledge of the quarry to be hunted, the terrain, and habitat are just the start. The birds themselves are remarkable creatures with their own complex behavior that must be studied in order for the team to be successful in the field. All this, in addition to a dedication toward the bird's care and well-being year-round, makes falconry a demanding yet rewarding sport.

In very general terms, falconry can be divided into two different forms: longwing and shortwing. This refers loosely to the different types of raptors. Longwing refers to true falcons such as the fabled peregrine, the prairie falcon, or the gyr falcon. Longwinging mostly involves the pursuit of avian quarry such as pheasant, ducks, or quail. It utilizes some of the most classic of falconry methods such as pointing dogs to locate game while the falcon waits on the falconer from high in the air. When birds are flushed, the falcon stoops, or dives, from high above.

Shortwings include members of the genus Buteo such as the red tailed hawk and the red-shouldered hawk, and also the true hawks of the genus Accipiter. Examples of these would be the goshawk and Cooper's hawk. Shortwingers often focus on ground quarry such as cottontails, hares, jackrabbits, and squirrels. Typically, man and hawk move through the cover searching for quarry. The hawk either stays on the fist or selects a perch over the falconer, often moving ahead on its own. Most birds soon learn that their human partner will often find game first. Although Accipiters, such as the gos and Cooper's hawk, are more than capable of pursuing avian prey, a large portion of shortwing falconry is oriented toward the pursuit of ground quarry.

I waited nearby and listened for signs of her success. As I approached the spot where she had disappeared into the undergrowth, I heard the familiar tinkling of her leg bells. I found her standing alone and empty handed. Between the hunter and the hunted, there are never any guarantees. The rabbit had won the day. I called her back to my fist. Unlike her totally wild counterpart, she would eat tonight, regardless of failure. Born in the wild, she could easily be returned there at the proper time, perhaps more confident and experienced than her wild siblings.

The sun was now an orange ball of fire sinking through the trees. I leashed her to my glove and we hiked toward the road. My game bag would be light this trip, but I was richer in one more memory of the hunt. "There will be other days," I told her as she stared at me. I smiled at the thought.

Some Natural History

Standing 18 to 25 inches (46 to 64 centimeters) with a wingspan up to 4 feet (1.2 meters) the red-tail is a large, stocky hawk. There are several color phases and subspecies. Typical light-phase birds have a whitish breast and a rust-colored tail. Young birds are duller, more streaked, essentially brown, and lacking the brick red-colored tail of the adults. Red-tailed hawks are distinguished from red-shouldered and Swainson's hawks by their stocky build; broader, more rounded wings; and white chest. This species is quite variable in color, especially in the West, where blackish individuals occur; certain western birds with grayish, faintly streaked or mottled tails were formerly considered a separate species called a Harlan's hawk. These other color morphs usually retain the characteristic rusty tail.

Red-tails inhabit deciduous forests and open country of various kinds, including tundra, plains, and farmlands. Upon nesting, two or three white, brown-spotted eggs are usually laid in a bulky nest of sticks lined with shreds of bark and bits of fresh green vegetation. The location is, more often than not, in a tall tree or on a rock ledge.

Their range is throughout North America, from Alaska east to Nova Scotia and southward. They winter across the United States north to southern British Columbia and the Maritime Provinces. The voice of the red-tail is recognized by a high-pitched descending scream with a hoarse, keeeeer. The red-tail is the most common and widespread American member of the genus Buteo, which also includes the red-shouldered, Swainson's, and gray hawks, among others. Like other hawks of this group, it soars over open country in search of its prey but, just as often, perches in a tree at the edge of a meadow, watching for the slightest movement in the grass below. Although often accused of it, the red-tailed hawk rarely takes poultry, but prefers feeding mainly on small rodents and mammals.

The Cooper's Hawk

When my son's legs got long enough, he sometimes tagged along with me on hunting trips. When he became old enough to legally hunt, we picked a sunny morning in early fall and went to one of my favorite wood lots. This location not only had an abundance of small game but was also a great place to see all kinds of wildlife.

This was one of those mornings you remember. We walked quietly into the wood lot and found a place to sit with our backs up against a big oak. A gray squirrel, angry at our in-

trusion, began to bark and chatter at us. After a time, we saw some movement down at the far end of the wood lot. A family group of four or five deer was moving down the edge of the woods. They didn't seem to be in any particular hurry, and their direction of travel brought them within 50 yards of us. This was one of the first opportunities for my son to see wild deer up close, and he was having a little trouble sitting still. The lead doe looked over in our direction and after a couple seconds seemed satisfied that whatever we were, we were not a threat. After the deer had picked their way down the edge of the wood lot out of sight, we remained under the oak and talked quietly about seeing the deer.

A few minutes later, my son alerted me to some more activity coming from the same direction that the deer had come from. It took us a couple of seconds to identify them through the early fall undergrowth, but we soon saw a big flock of turkeys headed down the same trail. The big birds did a little more wandering than the deer did, lingering longer in our part of the wood, scratching in the leaves, and making their quiet cutting sounds. This kind of thing can really test the patience of some youngsters, but I remember noting how he somehow managed to sit still enough so that we did not tip off the turkeys to our location as they leisurely fed by us. As the last of the flock wandered away, I smiled to myself as my son remarked in a whisper how he "sure wished it was turkey season."

The wood lot was full of big gray squirrels. I grew up hunting and eating small and large game of all kinds. I have tried to give my kids the same opportunities in a world much more disconnected from that sort of thing. Since squirrels were part of this morning's mission, when a big gray appeared from around the other side of an adjacent tree, I signaled for my son to get ready.

Just as he'd been taught, he waited for the squirrel's head to disappear down into the leaves as it foraged, before sliding the .22 rifle up on to his knee. Just as he began to settle in and wait for a shot, a large bird swooped in at a high rate of speed right between the unsuspecting gray squirrel and us.

We both saw the bird at the same time and, although it wasn't necessary, I whispered for Justin to wait.

The bird halted its initial attack just as it reached the squirrel, then veered off and perched on an old stump several feet from the feeding gray. It was then that I had an opportunity to identify the bird that had interrupted our hunt with its own.

The bird that had suddenly arrived on the scene was a juvenile Cooper's hawk. The bird was identifiable by its plumage, and its larger size probably made it a female of the species. What transpired next took perhaps no more than 3 or 4 minutes.

We noticed right away that the big gray squirrel had, up to this point, hardly looked up from its feeding. When the squirrel put its head down into the leaves, the Cooper's hawk launched another attack from its perch on the stump. Instantly, the squirrel turned and rushed the hawk as it flew toward it, chattering angrily. This unexpected behavior totally confused the young hawk, and it immediately retreated back to the stump. After a second or two, the squirrel turned and resumed its search through the leaf litter. After cocking its head and looking even more puzzled, the hawk launched a third *attack from directly behind, and instantly the big gray wheeled again and charged the hawk.*

I found what was occurring to be very interesting. The Cooper's hawk is considered to be pretty much an obligate bird-eating hawk in the eastern part of its range. This juvenile Coop was laboring under inexperience on the one hand and probably great hunger on the other. Although I'm quite certain that the Cooper's hawk feeds on other prey, including small rodents when it gets the opportunity, the young hawk's plan to catch and eat an adult gray squirrel was clearly a little too ambitious.

It always surprises many people to learn just how tough a customer the eastern gray squirrel is. Strong for its size and very agile, it is quite at home in its three-dimensional forest habitat. The larger hawks of North America hunt squirrels regularly, with the most notable being the red-tailed hawk, but the Cooper's is a significantly smaller and lighter hawk weighing sometimes less than an adult gray squirrel.

We sat motionless for the several minutes it took the drama to play out in front of us. The blatant disregard for the Cooper's hawk on the part of the squirrel was outright comical. It did, however, illustrate to me again how most prey animals have a keen ability for recognizing the particular kind of raptor they may encounter. Had this been a red-tail or goshawk, the gray would most certainly not have acted so blasé. After being thwarted a third time, the young hawk apparently gave up on squirrel for breakfast, and in a flash was gone through the trees.

I don't remember if we ever took any squirrels home that trip. I don't think it really mattered.

Wild Turkeys

A turkey? In town? People are always incredulous when they find out what it is they have been watching in their backyards. The wild turkey is a good example of a relative newcomer to the urban wildlife scene. The grasslands and agricultural fields of the 1960s and 1970s are largely gone now, replaced by a successional growth of dense brush and maturing trees. This condition, which helped cause the decline of the ring-necked pheasant, was tailor-made for the wild turkey. The early American colonists wrote about finding two different types of turkey in the new world. One had what they called a savory meat, and the other, according to most accounts, was all but inedible. It was later discovered that the inedible variety was actually the turkey vulture. By the end of the 19th century, the wild turkey had been hunted almost to extinction in much of its original range. Now with protection, restocking programs, and the return of the mature forests and secondary growth favored by turkeys, this species has made a remarkable comeback. The large amount of green space provided by modern subdivisions is easily taken advantage of by the wild turkey. Over 30 years ago, my first look at a wild turkey required a 3-hour drive into the southern tier of New York where most of the state's only populations of these birds existed. Today, I routinely take calls regarding these large birds from every suburb of Buffalo and have even rescued one from downtown.

The wild turkey belongs to the family Phasianidae, which also includes pheasants and grouse. The males can be quite large at 42 inches tall, and the females are 36 inches tall. The turkey's coloration is usually a dusky brown, barred with black, with an iridescent bronze sheen. The head and neck are naked, with bluish and reddish wattles. The tails are fan shaped, with chestnut, buff, or white tail tips. Males have spurs and a long beard on the breast. Females are smaller, and they lack the spurs and beard.

The wild turkey's range is much of the United States from Arizona east, and as far north as New England. It was introduced to many western states, including California. Throughout its range, the wild turkey is comprised of several subspecies.

Males produce gobbling calls similar to those of domestic turkeys. Hens produce a series of yelps, clucks, and cutting sounds.

Although wild turkeys were well known to American Indians and widely used by them as food, certain tribes considered these birds stupid and cowardly, and did not eat them for fear of acquiring these characteristics. They are now common in areas where they were totally absent a few decades ago. Turkeys are swift runners and quite wary. They often roost over water because of the added protection that this location offers. They are polygamous, and the male gobbles and struts with tail fanned to attract and hold his harem.

Wild turkeys eat a variety of food items ranging from hard mast such as acorns and beech and hickory nuts, to agricultural foods such as corn and soybeans. They can often be found in spring and summer hunting grasshoppers and other insects in open meadows.

Wild turkeys are becoming increasingly more common in the suburbs. There are still many folks whose first introduction to this species is finding one or more in their backyard. Many are not prepared for how large these birds really are, and how seemingly comfortable they can be foraging under the bird feeder or catching grasshoppers and other insects in the grass. Typically, wildlife rehabilitators and game officials get calls or complaints from the public starting in April when turkeys begin their breeding behavior. This can go on through June, depending on what area of the country you live in; the birds just start showing up in the open more and more. In the suburbs, showing up in the open can mean appearing anywhere from a backyard or a golf course to the nearest street intersection. They have been known to stop traffic.

Turkeys communicate by sight and sound. Their visual acuity is almost raptor-like, and they can spot other turkeys from great distances. They also hear very well and vocalize to each other quite a bit during the spring, with hens yelping to locate other hens and, more importantly, the male gobblers. And as one might imagine gobblers, well, they gobble! This lets hens know they are interested and also informs potential male rivals that they are in charge. When breeding season peaks in the turkey world, these birds can act much like deer in that they will sometimes ignore all other outside stimuli in the quest to procreate. This can make them behave well, for lack of a better term, goofy. If we can all just remember back to when we started getting interested in the opposite sex, it should be easier to cut them a little slack.

The nature of turkey complaints can range from fear for the birds' safety near the roadway to the uninformed notion that the birds are somehow "lost." I hear this a great deal from people who discover wildlife where they least expect it.

Wildlife doesn't get lost. Wildlife is everywhere today. It isn't so much the fact that it is everywhere, as it is how we respond to it. Turkeys are fascinating birds. They are, of course, harmless to humans and of great benefit to the environment in their insect-eating ability.

Great Blue Heron

Many decades ago, my grandfather and uncle built a cabin on a secluded Adirondack lake. It remains in the family today, and in the past, we have enjoyed several fishing trips to one of the last places in New York State that could pass for wilderness.

Like at many lakes in this region, the numbers of fish and other wildlife that live there can be astounding. In those days, we would use canoes or small skiffs with nothing bigger than an electric trolling motor for power. This lake was a veritable pan fish factory, and there were times the fishing could get fast and furious.

My wife and I had anchored our little 14-foot canoe on the downwind side of one of the tiny islands in the center of the lake, and we were busy crappie fishing. For those of you who don't fish (or eat fish someone else has caught), crappie are probably one of the best eating fish in North America. They are known by many names. They are also great fun to catch. The lake holds several warm-water species but is known for its crappie, or calico bass, population. Fishing had been slow thus far this particular trip, but with the coming of a warm gentle rain, a school of crappie came up from the depths and into the shallow cove to begin their spawning activities. Our bobbers started disappearing as fast as we set them out.

After a half hour or so of fishing, I took a break and happened to look over my shoulder to see a great blue heron land on a half-submerged tree that had fallen into the water. The fishing was pretty good for him too. We watched him spear several small fish with his long beak and gulp them down. Just then my wife pulled in a small crappie that had managed to completely swallow her lure. We had the necessary tools in our fishing tackle to safely remove hooks and always made every effort to release small fish unharmed. This time we were unable to get the hook out cleanly, and it was soon obvious the undersize fish would not survive. The fish was too small to clean for human consumption, and I was about to suggest we place it on the stringer anyway in order not to waste it, when we suddenly got an idea.

After coasting in closer to shore, we pitched the fish up onto the bank as close to the heron as possible. It landed with a splat right at the shoreline. After watching us back our canoe out a little ways, the big bird immediately flew over to where the hapless little fish lay and without hesitation speared it, flipped it up, and down the hatch it went. We couldn't resist— after that and over the next hour, any crappie that didn't meet our self-imposed size limit, was immediately flipped up on shore and happily recycled by our new fishing partner.

That much of the story is a fond memory in itself, but the best part was that bright and early next morning as we motored back toward the little island, a glance over my shoulder revealed a great blue heron flying about 150 yards directly behind the boat, shadowing us across the lake.

Heron Depredation

One of the trends these days for the American homeowner is the ornamental pond. With whole books written on the subject, and various pre-fab liners and kits readily available, it is possible to create an aquatic oasis in your backyard almost overnight.

Along with this popularity comes the inclination for many folks to stock these ponds with fish. Some prefer simple goldfish; others choose more exotic (and expensive) fish like koi, which are essentially fancy carp with a pedigree.

This is all well and good, and we certainly have the right to make our property look and feel the way we want. However, right along with this trend to bring a little wetland into our backyards comes the great blue heron. A predatory fish eater and a skilled hunter, this large wading bird is quick to realize what an easy meal looks like. You see, most people who build these small ornamental ponds do not think to provide the fish with anything in the way of a refuge should a predator show up. Natural ponds, lakes, and streams have cover such as rocks, vegetation, etc., where prey species can hide. Not unlike on dry land in the forest where all creatures inhabit their own niche. For the herons, it is literally like shooting fish in a barrel. It is not uncommon for one or more herons to completely clean out an ornamental pond of any and all fish in short order.

As it turns out, there are a couple very effective methods that, if used together, can all but eliminate the problem of a heron cleaning out your pond. Most pond liners are black. This makes it even easier for the herons that, like all birds, see color. Fish show up really well against the black backdrop.

First, get some plastic milk crates. If your pond is shallow and you're worried about aesthetics, choose black ones. Tip them upside down and sink them into your pond. If they don't want to sink well, put a nice attractive rock on top. (The rock actually makes this look better anyway.) What this does is provide cover for your fish. When threatened by a predator, the fish will learn to naturally retreat into the protective confines of the milk crate. When the coast is clear, they will tend to roam, and then can be enjoyed by anyone viewing the pond. Are the fish too big for the holes in the milk crate? Simply make the hole bigger with some utility shears or a razor knife. This method also helps depredation by other pond raiders such as raccoons.

The second phase of the project involves a few dollars, but nothing like the cost of four or five nice koi or large fancy goldfish. Find out which large sporting goods chain in your area sells duck decoys like the kind used by waterfowl hunters. Once there, ask if they have in stock or can order a plastic heron effigy. A plastic heron, when used in a spread of duck decoys, is referred to as a confidence builder to help put wary ducks at ease when flying into a spread of decoys.

Oddly enough, the presence of the fake heron has just the opposite effect on any real herons flying over your pond. Herons are largely solitary hunters. The amount of fish they need dictates that. On small bodies of water, one heron is enough, and more often than not, any heron flying near will keep on going. Move the effigy every other day or so.

This large wading bird stands 39 to 52 inches (99 to 132 centimeters) with a wingspan of 5 feet 10 inches (1.8 meters). The great blue heron is considered a common, large, mainly grayish heron with a pale or yellowish bill. Often mistaken for a sandhill crane, it flies with its neck folded, not extended like that of a crane. In southern Florida an all-white form, the great white heron, differs from the great egret in being larger, with greenish-yellow rather than black legs.

Herons can be found just about anywhere in lakes, ponds, rivers, and marshes.

Nesting behavior consists of three to seven pale greenish-blue eggs placed on a shallow platform of sticks lined with finer material, usually in a tree, but sometimes on the ground or concealed in a reedbed. The birds congregate to nest in colonies.

As far as range, it breeds locally from coastal Alaska, south-central Canada, and Nova Scotia south to Mexico and the West Indies. Herons winter as far north as southern Alaska, the central United States, and southern New England. They can also be found in the Galapagos Islands.

Their voice can be described as a harsh squawk.

These adaptable birds' large size enables them to feed on a variety of prey: from large fish and frogs to mice, small birds, and insects. The great blue heron has one of the widest ranges of any North American heron. This wide choice of food enables it to remain farther north during the winter than other species, wherever there is open water. However, such lingering birds may fall victim to severe weather. Most great blue herons nest in colonies in tall trees; their presence is often unsuspected until the leaves fall and the groups of saucer-shaped nests are exposed to view. In late summer, young herons disperse widely and may be encountered at small ponds, in mountain waters, or even in backyard pools, wherever fish are plentiful.

Ducks and Other Waterfowl

The increase in the numbers of waterfowl in the past few decades has significantly affected human recreational activities. Many ducks and geese no longer traditionally migrate, but rather stay in close proximity to urban green space where water, food, and nesting cover are plentiful. The resultant droppings and aggressive nest-guarding behavior can sometimes prove an annoying challenge for golfers, picnickers, and playground kids.

Geese

Many municipalities have had success in discouraging nuisance geese with streamers of red Mylar tape attached to posts sticking into the ground around the circumference of a pond or lake. The geese find the red color and flashing movement unsettling and often leave. Others have covered smaller bodies of water with netting that denies the birds' access to the water, forcing them to find a more suitable habitat. Predator effigies can sometimes work to reduce or prevent geese from small ponds and the surrounding grass. One of the most popular these days is the floating alligator head effigy. One or two of these on a small pond can keep geese suspicious enough to stay out of the area.

Certain landscaping techniques can be used to make a pond area less attractive to geese. For example, rather than cutting grass all the way to the water's edge, some property owners and developers have learned that ringing a pond or a small lake with boulders at the shoreline make it difficult for geese to utilize the habitat in the same way. Geese are large, heavy-bodied birds and, like most wildlife, would rather take the path of least resistance in moving about. Boulders and rip-rap at the water's edge make it difficult for geese to get in and out of the water easily. They can always land on the water, but they are grazers and sooner or later need the grass. The rocks provide a constant barrier that needs to be negotiated every time. Plus, the geese instinctively know the rocks have the potential to hide predators. In addition, alternate plantings of ground cover, such as pachysandra over bladed grasses, are much less desirable to geese as a food source and serve to help make the area much less attractive in terms of a feeding area.

One of the most innovative methods of the last few years that have proven successful is the use of trained dogs, such as border collies and Australian shepherds, to routinely visit these problem areas and harass geese before nesting season, causing them to choose a more private nesting location.

One of the best kept secrets for keeping geese and other waterfowl off the grass is heavily concentrated grape Kool-Aid. Mix it with water, but without added sugar, and put it in a garden sprayer. It must be applied liberally and more frequently when it rains, but for a manageable size piece of ground, it can be one more tool to consider.

Ducks

Mallard ducks are common residents these days in cities and suburbs.

These birds are quite at home nesting and raising their brood right out in full view of people and pets; sometimes perilously close to danger of all kinds. It is a fact of life that many ducklings do not survive to adulthood. Traffic, uncontrolled pets, and natural predators take their toll on the often large broods of young, and yet some waterfowl populations are still at an all time high. If you have a family of mallards or other waterfowl living on, traveling through, or nesting on your property, please realize that it is often a temporary situation that will change as the baby ducks grow.

Every year I'm contacted by many folks who are concerned about female ducks walking around the cities and suburbs with their young in tow. Usually, the desire is that the baby ducks be "relocated" to a safer environment. This course of action is fraught with some logistical and ethical problems. Consider the fact that the wild or rural mallard ducks have statistically more natural predators than their suburban and urban cousins. Snapping turtles, large fish, various birds of prey, etc., can all impact ducklings. Those ducks that inhabit the cities and suburbs have more traffic and domestic pets to negotiate. There is no "safer" place to relocate these young waterfowl to. Even so, attempts to capture the entire family often go unrewarded with would-be rescuers ending up scattering the family of ducks, thus putting the young at an even higher risk.

Ducks in Swimming Pools

Every year, many people have issues with resident mallard ducks invading their swimming pools. This behavior actually begins long before the pool is opened for the season. The key to what is occurring most of the time is the stagnant water that is allowed to collect on the pool cover during the off-season. Let's look at this from the ducks' point of view.

Mallards are known as puddle ducks. In other words, they are attracted to small amounts of standing water. Typically, what the homeowner or pool maintenance company does is lower the water level and then cover the pool. It is desirable, from a pool maintenance angle, to have the cover contacting or very close to the surface of the water. This tends to keep leaves and other debris from entering the pool during the winter months.

This plan goes awry when the pool cover collects rain water or snowmelt and, over time, grows algae and other pond life. This is exactly the kind of habitat that is exploitable by mallards. Most people do not understand how habituated the ducks become to swimming and feeding in the pool covers during the early spring. They are often reluctant to leave once the pool is opened for the summer. Even though the pool no longer contains a viable food source, the pool is viewed by the ducks as a safe habitat. They can easily trade back and forth to other areas where food is available and return to the pool for safety from predators. In addition, the female, or hen mallard, often chooses this locale to nest and hatch her brood of ducklings. If able, she then takes them into the pool to swim and feed, not realizing that the ducklings might not be able to get out on their own. One problem now becomes two.

Control of this scenario can begin with some modification to the pool covering scheme. One way is through the use of inner tubes left floating on top of the water before the pool cover is installed. This significantly reduces the amount of water that can collect in the pool cover, thus reducing the habitat available to the ducks.

Additional securing of the pool cover is often required with the use of this method, but the pay-off is little or no duck activity around the pool.

Some people choose to be vigilant and routinely keep any water pumped out of the cover during the off-season. There are pool covers available that stretch and remain taut. These are often made of a permeable material that allows rain and snowmelt to pass through while keeping debris out. They sometimes use a system of struts or supports underneath. These covers are often more expensive initially but can save work and frustration later on. In-ground pool owners can approximate this design by nailing pressure-treated two-by-fours together so that they span the width of the pool on edge, and using them to support a less expensive vinyl cover. Raising the cover up a little higher on one end will help keep it drained. When I suggest these relatively simple methods to pool owners, many are appreciative and try them with much success. Other pool owners immediately start citing reasons why they can't use these methods or that they won't work. These are usually the people I end up talking to in June, who are sick of having ducks land in their pool.

Ducklings trapped in the pool should be retrieved with the pool skimmer and placed in a recycling bin or other suitable container. Ignore all the fussing and scare tactics of the hen for the moment. When all the babies are captured, begin walking away from the pool. The mother duck will generally follow you in an attempt to rescue her young. If she remains behind, gently pick up one of the ducklings and show it to her. This is usually all it takes for her to follow you away from the pool and out of the area. Release the young in sight of the hen and they should all immediately form up, gather around their mother, and march off. Do not expect a thank you.

Geese

The Canada goose can be described as a large waterfowl 35 to 45 inches tall. It has a brownish body with a black head, long black neck, and a conspicuous white cheek patch. The smaller brant has a shorter neck and lacks the white cheek patch. The cackling goose is smaller, darker, shorter-billed, and found mainly in the West.

Their preferred habitat includes lakes, bays, rivers, and marshes. They often feed in open grasslands and stubble fields.

Nests contain four to eight whitish eggs in a large mass of grass and moss lined with down, usually on the ground near water or on a muskrat lodge, but sometimes in a tree in an abandoned osprey or bald eagle nest.

Their breeding range is from Alaska east to Baffin Island in the far north, and south to California, Illinois, and Massachusetts. They winter as far south as northern Mexico and the Gulf Coast. Canada geese are very widespread as a semi-domesticated bird in city parks and on reservoirs.

Well known for their V-shaped migrating flocks and rich, musical honking, Canada geese are among the most familiar of North America's waterfowl. In earlier times there were formerly 11 subspecies recognized geographically, but the smaller races have recently been established as a separate species, called the cackling goose (B. hutchinsonii). The larger forms, ranging in size from the giant Canada goose of the northern prairies to the much smaller lesser Canada goose, remain grouped together. The most commonly seen variety is the one that nests south of the Hudson Bay, which numbers well over 1 million. As with all geese, these birds are chiefly grazers, feeding on stubble fields, grasses, and other vegetation. Over the last few decades they have become increasingly tolerant of humans, and many Canada geese choose to nest in city parks and suburbs. They are especially noticeable in late summer and early fall when they form large flocks on golf courses and large lawns; at such times, they have come to be regarded as pests.

The coyote is another suburban resident common to most areas of North America. They are canines, belonging to the same family as wolves and foxes. They have adapted themselves to every type of habitat in North America. Coyotes are found in the wooded area and brushy drainages of the Northeast, the warm swampy south, the arid western regions, and even the subarctic tundra. Their increase in numbers has been sparking some controversy. According to many naturalists and wildlife biologists, the coyote has been moving into the area of the Great Lakes since the 1940s. Other areas of the eastern United States report a similar history. This intelligent and highly adaptable animal has not needed man's help at all to increase its range throughout the United States.

Although technically a carnivore, it is well documented that coyotes subsist quite well on just about anything in the plant or animal kingdom. It is much easier to list what a coyote won't eat than what it will. Though uncommon, it is documented that coyotes will attack family pets if given the opportunity. This should not cause as much concern for the presence of coyotes in our neighborhoods as it should for keeping our cats indoors and our dogs on leashes. This is something all of us as responsible pet owners should be doing every day.

The coyote's innate ability to size up a situation can sometimes get it into trouble. Small to medium-sized dogs chained outside, for example, can sometimes draw the attention of coyotes that seem to be able to discern that the dog can't escape. This has provoked an occasional attack. This can also include small dogs in outdoor kennels. A coyote's interest in domestic dogs runs the gamut from social or sexual to outright predatory behavior. It can start out one way and end up quite another. If we're not providing some form of attraction, most of the time coyotes will give us and our property a wide berth. The same rules apply as for other nuisance wildlife. Storing trash properly and not leaving any pet food outside goes a long way. Coyotes encountered while we're out hiking or walking the dog will most likely be gone in a flash. The overly curious one that hangs around should be looked directly at, and spoken to in a loud voice. Removing coyotes should be seriously thought through before attempting. Consider the fact that man has tried eradicating the coyote from its western range for almost 100 years with no success. In actuality, studies show that coyotes significantly increase their reproduction under pressure.

Coyotes mate for life, and the pair bonding that occurs is still largely a mystery. In general, breeding takes place from February through March, and pups are born April to May. Both adults assist in rearing the young with the male playing an important role in protection and food supply until the pups can fend for themselves, usually at about 9 to 10 months.

Many deer hunters insist that the coyote has had significant impact on deer herds. Wildlife biologists will say that there is always predation of deer by coyotes, but ordinarily it is the very young or the very old and sick deer. This kind of predation is way more beneficial to a deer herd than a detriment. The truth is there are infinitely easier ways for a coyote to make a living than chasing healthy deer around. Nonetheless, we should not forget the tough and adaptable nature of these creatures.

November 2002

High winds are one of the worst conditions for bow hunting. There is nothing good about it. Shooting can be difficult to downright impossible; it seems to crank the deer up making them even more nervous, and it's no fun to sit in a tree that's swaying back and forth.

Fortunately the pressure-treated wooden platform I was perched in was very solid and well maintained. The early dawn hours had been calm enough, but the wind had picked up steadily and was gusting to about 25 to 30 miles per hour. Needless to say, I didn't expect a great deal of deer activity until the wind calmed. I was thinking of getting down and going for a walk when a flash of white off to my left caught my eye. The little yearling doe was hauling the mail when she passed by me. Her feet barely seemed to touch the ground between the 12-foot leaps she was making. Instinctively I followed her with my bow but at the same time knew there would be no opportunity. As she disappeared from view, out of habit I glanced in the direction from which she had come.

My eyes caught movement just in time to make out the shape of the large female coyote as she skulked off. This particular animal had a very blonde colored coat. I recognized her immediately as a coyote I had seen before. There was no snow on the ground so this deer was not hampered in any way except one: the wind. With the wind blowing the way it was, it must have been extremely difficult for the deer to hear. In addition, high winds can carry an animal's scent away from ground level where it is easily detected. I marveled at the coyote's ability to perceive the deer's handicap, and then attempt to stalk her under the cover of a stiff wind.

We need to remember that the coyote is a predator and will do what it needs to do to survive. However, in reality, the vast majority of a coyote's diet consists of small rodents, rabbits, and whatever seasonal plant growth it can find. The list of what a coyote will eat is one of the largest in the animal world. Rarely seen by people, coyotes are quite at home living in close proximity to humans. My family and I enjoy the odd occasion when the neighborhood pack hunts close to our house and begins their strange howling and screaming. I can't imagine a world without these intelligent canines. It would be a less wild one for sure, and that would be a pity.

Chance Encounter

Before my wife and I began fishing together a great deal, I would occasionally canoe by myself. Sliding quietly in a canoe on flat, calm water is something that has to be experienced to be appreciated. Not only is it a great way to fish, but the amount of quality bird and wildlife watching you can do is quite amazing.

One summer evening, I had a couple hours free before dark and, after sliding my canoe in at the boat launch; I paddled up a small tributary off the main branch of Oak Orchard Creek.

The sun was sinking slowly behind the trees as I rounded a bend. Up ahead, about 100 yards in the gloom, something was moving on top of the water.

Try as I might, for the life of me, I could not identify this creature. I remember thinking to myself that it looked like one of those little furry creatures from the movie 'Gremlins', having a tiny little body with disproportionately big ears.

Slowly, as I got close, it became clear that the strange creature was a white-tailed doe up to her neck in the water. Only her head was visible, with the rest of her body completely submerged. As the canoe glided closer, I thought that something was odd about this. All the deer that I had ever seen swimming rode a little higher in the water than this.

I have a healthier respect and caution these days for deer than I did back then. I don't fear whitetail; on the contrary, I love them. I love to watch them, study them, and hunt them; and my family looks forward to the venison every season. But my years in animal rescue and wildlife rehabilitation have taught me to exercise extreme caution when approaching a live white-tailed deer. They are powerful animals and, if need be, are capable of defending themselves. In those days, however, like most young men, I rarely thought about the consequences of my actions.

I slid the canoe up alongside the deer, which seemed to be having some trouble swimming. She didn't seem to be in panic mode but did try to put some distance between herself and the boat. I had no trouble keeping up with her. I shudder a little when I think of what could have happened to me in my little fiberglass canoe, literally sitting right next to a trapped whitetail in the water. After observing her for a couple minutes, I noticed that her hind legs were just hanging limp beneath her. It suddenly dawned on me what had probably happened to her. It was quite likely she had been hit by a car and either ran or rolled down the steep banks of the creek into the water. Once in the water, she had become trapped not only by the steep banks of the creek but also by an inability to use her hind legs.

It was, as they say, a weird scene. The deer was in quite a pickle and yet strangely she didn't seem really upset. With me sitting in a boat right next to her, the whole scene seemed a little surreal. I don't know if she had figured out in her little mind that she had bigger problems than me or not.

I sat with her for a while trying to figure out if there was something I could do for her, but all I had was my canoe paddle and a fishing pole. This was long before the golden age of cell phones, so I was unable to either put her out of her misery or call for help. Plus, we were a mile up the creek with no one in sight. After a time, I wished her well and went on my way. Later that evening, returning to the landing in near darkness, I didn't see her. A week or so later, I did come upon the floating carcass of a deer in the same stretch of water. I assumed it was her, and it made me a little sad to think of her hopeless struggle for survival.

Fawns

Every year I talk with people regarding white-tailed deer. In the springtime, the majority of those calls have to do with fawns.

Early in the fawn's life, the doe periodically stashes her young in what she deems a suitable place. The fawn generally stays put, motionless most of the time, while the mother leaves the area to feed, bed, and chew her cud. Newborn fawns give off little or no natural scent and so, by remaining motionless, are usually well protected from natural predators. Some time later, the doe returns to nurse and often, move the fawn. As the youngster grows, it begins to travel with the female more and more.

This amazing behavioral process can go awry many different ways. People and pets often happen upon the hidden fawn while out walking, hiking, or in the course of doing yard work. A natural human reaction is often the assumption that the fawn is aban- doned and needs help. Sometimes the fawn is actually in trouble. Does are periodically hit by cars while crossing the road. In this case, when mom doesn't show up on time, the fawn begins to vocalize out of hunger and/or begins to wander. There are those few individual fawns, which we see periodically, that do not be- have like the majority and wander and/or vocalize without really being in trouble. Fortunately these *"problem children"* are rare, and most fawns stay put until the doe gets back.

If after a period of time it appears that something has happened to the mother, a wildlife rehabilitator who specializes in the raising of white-tailed deer should be contacted if possible. In cases where there has been unnecessary human intervention, an attempt can be made to reunite the doe with the fawn. The latest technique I have utilized involves locating and attracting the doe through the use of a commercially available deer call, the type often used by deer hunters and nature photographers. Deer produce a number of different vocal sounds and communicate with each other often.

By reproducing the distress bleat of a fawn, we can often locate the doe and lure her close enough to see her fawn.

Reunion

The police officer was doing what he thought was best. In retrospect, it was probably a good decision. Most of the time I caution people to leave fawns where they are found, as most often the doe is in the immediate area, usually within a couple hundred yards. This fawn was found wandering on the edge of a busy expressway and brought to the wildlife rehab center. The chances of her getting hit by a car were high if she kept wandering. I asked the officer if he had noticed any dead deer near where he had picked up the fawn. He had thought the same thing and had looked carefully along the highway. He said no, he hadn't spotted anything along the shoulder of the road.

I was very familiar with the area where he found the fawn. There were several miles of chain link fence separating the highway from the bordering commercial and residential properties. I also knew that much of that chain link was in various stages of disrepair and had numerous openings along its length. It was common to see deer grazing along the fence line. It would be easy for a misbehaving fawn to get up and wander through the fence and not be able to get back across. I began to get more curious as we examined the fawn and she seemed too healthy. She did not appear to be a fawn that was missing a meal or two. There were no signs of any dehydration or stress at all. Indeed, her belly seemed rather full.

I mentally took stock of the situation. No dead deer sightings. A healthy fawn found in an area with man-made features conducive to separating a fawn from the adult. We loaded her up in a truck and I grabbed a deer call we keep for just such an occasion.

Luckily, the area where the fawn was found was accessible from the other side of the fence. Getting off at the nearest exit, we began to slowly cruise an industrial park immediately adjacent to where the officer had found the fawn wandering. We rolled down the truck windows, and while someone else took the wheel, I began to use the deer call. I adjusted the reed to reproduce the bleat of a fawn in distress. In my experience, after does drop their fawns they are very susceptible to the sound of fawn vocalizations. We got to the end of the commercial property without seeing any deer.

When we could go no further, we turned around and headed back nice and slow while I kept intermittently blowing on the call with my most convincing fawn bleat. Suddenly, out of the corner of my eye I caught a flash of white. I glanced over to see a big doe staring at us about 100 yards away. We threw the truck into park, jumped out, and grabbed the fawn out of the carrier in the back of the truck. Initially I had Gordy, one of our wildlife volunteers; hold the fawn while I began working the call again. At that moment the fawn herself began bleating, and upon hearing the real deal, the doe instantly began trotting toward us. When she broke into a run, I quickly began to think things over. We were about to have an upset whitetail in our lap that was more than capable of defending her offspring. Not only was Gordy a volunteer, but it was also his first day. I suddenly decided if someone was going to have to deal with a ticked-off mama whitetail, it might as well be me. I grabbed the fawn and told Gordy to back up and stay down low near the truck. By this time, mom was within 50 yards and had murder in her eye. Crouching low, I set the fawn down and pointed it in her direction. Some days every-

thing just goes right, I thought to myself, as the fawn scampered in her direction. Just then, mom leaped over the fawn and kept coming right at me.

Needless to say, I hadn't planned on this reaction from the doe, and I leisurely mulled over my options for a second or two. If I stood up, displaying my upright human outline, and startled her bad enough, she might hightail it out of there and leave us with a tenuous, rather than a tight, hookup with the fawn. If I stayed low and didn't move, she might not really identify me until it was too late. I knew what she was capable of inflicting on me. Deciding on a compromise, I turned, stayed low, and beat feet for the safety of the truck. If you've ever watched any old Marx Brothers movies, all I can say is Groucho would've been proud of me as I half ran to the truck, bent over at the waist. The doe slowed her gait and finally stopped, suddenly more concerned with the fawn. We got in the truck, turned the key, and made our getaway. As we drove off, we saw the doe headed back into the brush with the fawn wobbling behind her. As we headed back Gordy said, "That's the most amazing thing I ever saw." I shuddered and said, "Yeah, some days everything goes just right."

Feeding Deer: Exploring the Myths

Feeding white-tailed deer has become an emotionally charged issue. Let's reduce this to two basic myths and see how they hold up in the light of the truth.

Myth #1: *Because we have fed them so long, they are dependent on us.*

Actually, deer are remarkably adaptive, opportunistic creatures and, like many other species, are capable of changing their behavior as food supplies come and go. Ask any farmer and they will tell you that as seasonal crops dwindle, deer turn their attentions toward other food sources. These food sources are not always obvious to us.

Myth #2: *In winter, there is nothing for the deer to eat.*

As the season turns colder, deer switch from eating lush plant growth to what we call browse. Browse is defined as any one of a number of varieties of woody plant materials in the form of shrubs, bushes, and saplings. This is the type of food their digestive systems are adapted to use during the colder months.

Feeding foods high in carbohydrates such as alfalfa, corn, bakery products, and other processed foods provides poor nutrition that deer's digestive systems are not adapted to use. The deer can actually spend more energy than they get, trying to digest these things. This can result in a live, but otherwise unhealthy, deer. Unhealthy deer that wouldn't normally survive, sooner or later raise unhealthy young, which ultimately increases deer populations to a number that can no longer be supported by a given piece of habitat.

Deer are not like dogs, cats, or domestic cattle. They are complex creatures with a life cycle deeply connected to the land and seasons. We have a responsibility to treat them correctly even if that means leaving them alone, while keeping in mind that doing the right thing doesn't always feel good.

Deer Facts

Size varies greatly in whitetails. Their coloration varies somewhat with the seasons, being tan or reddish brown in the summer and grayish brown in the winter. Belly, throat, nose band, eye ring, and inside of ears are white. Their tails are brown, edged with white above, often with a dark stripe down the center. The underside of the tail is white, and they have black spots on the sides of the chin. A buck's antlers have main beams forward, several unbranched tines behind, and small brow tines, with an antler spread of up to 3 feet (90 centimeters). The doe rarely has antlers.

The white-tailed deer population has become a public-health concern with the onset of Lyme disease, which is transmitted by ticks sometimes carried by the deer. These ticks are tiny and their nymphs are almost microscopic; both nymphs, active May through July, and adults, active on warm days from August through May, can be infectious. They inhabit woods and fields, especially where deer are numerous, and occur on both deer and mice. Lyme disease is a dangerous bacterial illness. Initial symptoms vary, but about 75 to 80 percent of all victims develop a circular, expanding, bulls-eye-shaped red rash around the tick bite, up to 35 days after the bite. Other symptoms include stiff neck, headache, dizziness, fever, sore throat, muscle aches, joint pain, and general weakness. Antibiotics are most effective in the early stages of infection. Untreated Lyme disease can be difficult to cure and may cause chronic arthritis, memory loss, and severe headaches.

The reproductive season for deer varies: it occurs in the first 2 weeks of November in the North, and in January or February in the South. One to three young are born after a gestation of about 6½ months.

Deer habitat includes farmlands, brushy areas, woods, suburbs, and gardens. Their range encompasses the southern half of the southern tier of Canadian provinces, and most of the United States, except the far Southwest.

Although primarily nocturnal, the white-tailed deer may be active at any time. It often moves to feeding areas along established trails, then spreads out to feed. The animal usually beds down near dawn, seeking concealing cover. This species is a good swimmer. The winter coat of the northern deer has hollow hair shafts, which fill with air, making the coat so buoyant that it would be difficult for the animal to sink should it become exhausted while swimming. The white-tailed deer is also a graceful runner, with top speeds up to 36 miles per hour, although it flees to nearby cover rather than run great distances. This deer can make vertical leaps of 8½ feet (2.6 meters) and horizontal leaps of 30 feet (9 meters). The white-tailed deer grazes on green plants, including aquatic ones in the summer; eats acorns, beechnuts, and other nuts and corn in the fall; and browses on woody vegetation in winter, including the twigs and buds of viburnum, birch, maple, and many conifers. The total list of plant life that a whitetail will eat numbers well over 100 varieties. Its four-part stomach allows the deer to feed on items that most other mammals cannot eat. It can obtain nutrients directly from the food, as well as nutrients synthesized by microbes in its digestive system. Whitetails eat 5 to 9 pounds of food per day and drink water from rain, snow, dew, or other water sources.

When nervous, the white-tailed deer snorts through its nose and stamps its hooves, sending a telegraphic signal that alerts other nearby deer to danger. If alarmed, the deer flags, or raises, its tail, exhibiting a large, bright flash of white. This very visual signal communicates danger to other deer and helps fawns to follow their mothers in flight. There are two types of social groupings: the family group of a doe and her young, which remains together for nearly a year (and sometimes longer), and the buck group. The family group usually disbands just before the next birth, though occasionally two sets of offspring are present for short periods. Bucks are more social than does for most of the year, forming buck groups of three to five individuals. The buck group, which constantly changes and disbands shortly before the fall rut, is structured as a dominance hierarchy. Threat displays include stares, lowered ears, and head-up and head-down postures. Attacks involve kicking and, less commonly, rearing and flailing with the forefeet. Bucks and does herd separately most of the year, but in winter they may gather together, or yard up. As many as 150 deer may herd in a yard. Yarding keeps the trails open through the movement of large groups of animals and provides protection from predators.

The social structure of whitetails is matriarchal. Deer may occupy the same home range year after year and may defend bedding sites, but otherwise they are not territorial. The extended rutting season begins at about the time the male is losing his velvet, which varies with latitude. At this time, bucks are still in buck groups, and sparring for dominance increases. Sparring consists of two deer trying to push each other backward. The buck group then breaks up, and several bucks begin following a doe at a distance of 150 feet (50 meters) or so. They follow the doe's scent; the largest buck stays closest to the female. A buck attempts to dominate other bucks and may mate with several does over the breeding season. He produces buck rubs and also scrapes, revisiting them regularly during the rut; glandular secretions are left on the rubs. Does visit the scrapes and urinate in them; bucks then follow the trails of the does.

After the mating season, the doe returns to the sub-herd until spring (May or June in the North; January to March in the Deep South). A young doe bred for the first time usually produces one fawn, but thereafter has twins and occasionally triplets if food is abundant. The female remains near the fawns, returning to feed them only once or twice a day. Twin fawns are separated, which serves to protect them. Weaning occurs between 1 and 2½ months of age. Fawns stay with the mother into the fall or winter, some-times for up to 2 years, but the doe generally drives off her young of the previous year shortly before giving birth. The whitetail's first antlers are usually single spikes (spike horns). A 3-year-old would be expected to have eight points, but there can be more or less because the number of tines is influenced greatly by nutritional factors. A whitetail's age is determined not by the number of tines on its antlers but by the wear of its teeth.

Nuisance Deer Problems

As with all wildlife, there are those rare instances when deer can negatively impact crops and landscaping. Usually when crops are affected, it is an area where hunting is legal, and careful removal of excess deer can provide the best solution. Increasingly within the suburbs, however, hunting is becoming impractical due to human and animal population densities, safety, and sadly, nega-tive public opinion. When this occurs, controlling deer depreda-tion can be a challenge. As with other species, it is often best to consider a multi-faceted approach.

Fencing can provide varied results. On the positive side, deer often do not attempt to jump fencing that they cannot see through, and so, stockade type designs can be useful. Chain link is merely an unyielding form of vegetation to whitetails, and they will seek to cross it in order to gain access to food or cover. However, chain link in excess of 6 feet can begin to be a deterrent. Deer are capable of jumping higher but are not always willing to make the effort. Fencing that is installed to angle sharply outward from the area to be protected has proven to be effective as it seems to provide an obstacle that baffles the deer's attempts to jump it. An alternate method is to install an angled wire barrier atop an already existing chain link fence.

Chemical repellants can also deter deer from feeding on plantings. This method is often limited by cost factors when treating large areas. Combining appropriate fencing with repellants can often provide the necessary level of results. In areas where it is legal, allowing controlled hunting adjacent to fenced areas can often be the answer. Some people are beginning to experiment with motion activated devices like sprinklers, noise makers, etc. The cost of some of these devices can be quite high. Careful consideration should be made as to the size of the problem, costs, legalities, etc., before putting a comprehensive control plan together.

Gray Fox

The natural world is quite capable of teaching many lessons to those of us willing to pay attention. I find that many of us are quick to make assumptions regarding wildlife. I speak to hundreds of people annually, and too often I hear folks speaking in absolutes. Statements like "This animal is out during the day so it must be sick" or "I have never seen this type of behavior before, so something must be wrong with it" seem all too common these days.

Even those of us animal people can be guilty of jumping to conclusions. We tend to fill in the blanks without stopping to keep in mind that it is difficult, if not impossible, to know or predict every aspect of an animal's behavior. As I've said before, about the biggest mistake one can make regarding animals is using the words always, definitely, or never.

An animal control officer from one of the nearby suburbs brought an unconscious fox into the wildlife center one late fall day. It appeared to be in good physical shape with no outward signs of illness, hair loss, etc. He related to me how he had arrived at the home of a concerned resident who had observed the animal in a tree. After hearing his account of the call, apparently he had decided to capture the fox because it was "stuck in a tree." He subsequently shot the fox with a chemical immobilization dart. He related to me how, after observing the fox in the tree, it was obvious to him that this was abnormal behavior because according to him, a fox lives on the ground.

As it turns out, he was only partially correct. This fox was in fact a gray fox. Had it been a red fox, it would have been somewhat unusual to see it sitting in a tree, but for the gray fox, it was quite normal.

Grays are great climbers and spend a certain amount of time hunting in trees. This information is considered elementary to people who know a great deal about foxes, yet most folks are surprised when they learn of the gray foxes' penchant for tree climbing. We provided supportive care for the sleeping fox until he recovered and then took him back to his home range and released him.

There is never any shame in not knowing. But, it is assuming we know it all, which can form a barrier to learning and sometimes causes problems and excitement where there needn't be any.

Gray Fox Facts

The gray fox can be described as being colored a grizzled gray above, reddish on the lower sides, chest, and back of the head, with a white throat and belly. The tail is similarly colored, but has a black mane on top and a black tip. The legs and feet are rust colored. Grays have prominent ears. Their height is 14⅛ to 15 inches with a length averaging between 31 to 44 inches. They weigh between 7¼ to 13 pounds.

Breeding occurs between January and April. Usually one litter of one to seven young are born March through May. Gestation is 53 days. Habitats are varied, and are more often thicker and brushier than those of the red fox. They range throughout the eastern United States, east from eastern North and South Dakota, Nebraska, Kansas, and Oklahoma; and also in the West, in western Oregon, California, southern Nevada, southern Utah, Colorado, Arizona, New Mexico, and most of Texas.

Although active primarily at twilight and after dark, the common gray fox is sometimes seen foraging by day in brush, thick foliage, or timber. It is the only American canid with true climbing ability, often foraging in trees.

The common gray fox feeds heavily on cottontail rabbits, mice, voles, other small mammals, birds, insects, and much plant material, including corn, apples, persimmons, nuts, cherries, grapes, pokeweed fruit, grass, and blackberries. Grasshoppers, crickets, and other insects are often a very important part of the diet in late summer and autumn.

The gray fox favors den sites that include woodlands and spaces among boulders on the slopes of rocky ridges. This fox digs if necessary, and though it sometimes enlarges a woodchuck burrow, it often prefers to den in rocky clefts, small caves, rock piles, hollow logs, and hollow trees. Occupied during the breeding and whelping season, dens are seldom used the rest of the year. The male common gray fox helps tend the young but does not den with them. The young are weaned at 3 months and hunt for themselves at 4 months, when they weigh about 7 pounds. This fox growls, barks, or yaps, but is less vocal than the red fox. This species has few enemies. Bobcats, where abundant, may prey on gray foxes, and domestic dogs may kill a few. Rabies and distemper are important diseases.

Red Fox

I love to deer hunt from a tree stand. Sometimes I think it's just because I love sitting in trees. Spend enough time in the woods, and you will inevitably go through those times when things seem slow. With no deer sightings in a while, and not much other wildlife to occupy my interest, the afternoon was ticking by slowly that November day. It was late bow season in New York, and the local deer were conspicuous by their absence. After a couple of hours, I noticed some movement about 75 yards off to the right.

A big red fox was slipping quietly through the brush, apparently on a late afternoon hunt. More out of loneliness than any predatory nature on my part, I grabbed a deer call and adjusted the reed to reproduce a fawn's bleating. The fox was traveling parallel to my location and seemed intent on where it was going. I made a short, quavering bleat that interrupted the stillness of the afternoon. Instantly, the big vixen put the brakes on and looked my way. She thought it over for a couple seconds, then hung a left and came right toward my stand. It was easy to see the dramatic change in her demeanor as she stalked her way toward me. Every time she slowed down and began to search for the source of the "fawn," I let out another pitiful-sounding bleat. I wondered how long I could keep her fooled. It wasn't the deer hunt that I had planned, but then again, it wasn't boring either.

I eventually teased the big fox in to about 35 feet from where I sat concealed on a wooden platform in the branches of a scrubby little pine tree. Finally she hung up, sat back on her haunches, and tried to work it out. I could almost hear the wheels turning in her head. As with most four-footed predators, she most likely had a probable range-to-target stored in her little computer the first time I had called. But after closing the distance and not seeing, smelling, or hearing what she expected, her natural caution began to take over. We both sat there for a time, with her feeling perplexed and me admiring the afternoon sun on her thick red coat. After a while, I think it began to dawn on her that she had been had. My last good look at her was when she suddenly about-faced and snuck off in the direction she had come from. The tree stand I was perched in was at the edge of a small group of trees overlooking an open field. Scanning the field an hour or so later with my binoculars, I saw her again, mousing out in the middle of the goldenrod. I never saw a deer that day, but I appreciated Big Red's company nonetheless.

Red Fox Facts

This wild canid is easily identified. It is usually rusty reddish above with white under parts, chin, and throat. The long, bushy tail ends in a white tip. It has prominent pointed ears. The backs of its ears, lower legs, and feet are black. Color variations include a black phase (these are often almost completely black), a silver phase (black with silver-tipped hairs), a cross phase (reddish brown with a dark cross across the shoulders), and intermediate phases. All these color morphs have a white-tipped tail. Its height is 15 to 16 inches, and its length is 35 to 41 inches. The tail measures 13¾ to 17 inches. The red fox weighs in around 7 to 15 pounds.

Breeding behavior has foxes choosing mates from January into early March. One litter comprised of one to ten kits are born between March and May in a maternity den. Gestation is 51 to 53 days. Fox habitat varies from mixed cultivated and wooded tracts to thick brushy areas. Red foxes range throughout most of the United States and Canada, including the Northwest Territories, much of the western United States, and southern Florida.

Regarded as the embodiment of cunning, the red fox is believed by many field observers merely to be extremely cautious and, like other canids, capable of learning from experience. Suburban foxes, however, can become quite accustomed to the routines of their human neighbors. Often times they seem downright comfortable sitting in someone's backyard, waiting for an opportunity to steal the cat food off the back porch. Although possessing the ability to usually discern what we are up to, it wants nothing to do with humans, and its presence close by is rarely about a cause for concern. I believe that suburban foxes, or any foxes that have not been hunted or molested in any way by humans, begin to view us as just another large creature in their environment such as deer or cattle, etc. It eats whatever is available, feeding heavily in summer on vegetation, including corn, berries, apples, cherries, grapes, acorns, and grasses; and in winter on birds and mammals, including mice, rabbits, squirrels, and gophers. Invertebrates such as grasshoppers, crickets, caterpillars, beetles, and crayfish can compose up to one-fourth of its diet.

The hearing of the red fox differs from that of most mammals in that it is quite sensitive to low-frequency sounds. The fox listens and hones in on the underground digging, gnawing, and rustling sounds of small mammals. When it hears such sounds, it often rears up on its hind legs and pounces, frantically digging into the soil or snow to capture the animal. The red fox behaves like a cat in stalking its prey. When hunting larger quarry, such as rabbits, it stalks as close as possible, then attempts to run the prey down when it bolts.

An adult fox rarely retires to a den in winter. In the open, it curls into a ball, wrapping its bushy tail around its nose and foot pads, and at times may be completely blanketed with snow. Adults usually are solitary until the mating season, which begins (usually in late January or February) with nocturnal barking. The maternity den is established shortly after mating and abandoned by late August when families disperse. The female usually cleans out extra dens to be used in case of disturbance, but the same one may be occupied for several years. Upon birth, most pups already show the white tail tip. When about 1 month old, the young play above ground and feed on what is brought to them by their parents and sometimes by helper foxes: un-bred females or female progeny that have not left the territory. Food is given to the first pup that begs for it, and some young may die in seasons when food is scarce. At first, the mother predigests and regurgitates meat, but soon she brings live prey, enabling the kits to practice killing. Later the young begin to hunt with the parents. The kits disperse at about 7 months, with males traveling away up to 150 miles or more, but with females usually remaining closer. Adults also disperse, remaining solitary until the next breeding season.

Other than humans and automobiles, the red fox has few enemies except for rabies, mange, and distemper. In the mid-18th century, red foxes were imported from England and released in New York, New Jersey, Maryland, Delaware, and Virginia by landowners who enjoyed hunting them with hounds.

Opossums: And the Oscar goes to...

I would like to think I can remember the exact time in my life when I discovered something new outdoors. The truth is I can't. I can see it happening in my mind, but exactly when or how old I was—those details are fading now.

The winding country road I lived on was home to only a few youngsters my age. One of the only kids I hung around with lived down the road about a mile. My choices were usually to walk it or ride a bike. It was summer and the day was warming up fast. Sticking to the shoulder of the road, I was pedaling along when I spotted what looked like a crooked stick lying in my path up ahead. As I got closer, the "stick" began to move. It turned out to be a pretty big garter snake that was in the process of sunning itself on the warm pavement. Where I came from, catching snakes was considered a recreational pastime, and you never passed up the chance to get hold of one. Especially when you found one out in the middle of the road not paying any attention!

I hit the coaster brake, skidded to a stop, and was off the bike in a flash. The three-footer had sensed my approach and was already on its way into the ditch. I had a friend in school who also loved to catch garter snakes, and he was always yappin' to me about how he always caught the biggest snakes. In those days, you had to periodically bring one in to school in a coffee can in order to bolster your credibility. I knew this specimen would solidify my reign as master snake handler of my local elementary school, and so, I was hot on the snake's trail as it slithered into the tall grass at the side of the road. Out of the corner of my eye, I saw some reeds move in the bottom of the dry ditch. This was way too much disturbance for the average snake to make, so I halted my pursuit.

Peering into the clump of reeds, I spotted a patch of light gray fur. When I saw that it wasn't moving, I crept a little closer. It was an opossum. I don't remember ever seeing one up close before that time. I immediately assumed it had been hit by a car. Although I can't recall noticing any blood or trauma, it sure didn't look so good. It was about the size of a big cat, lying on its side, mouth open, and tongue hanging out. It smelled bad too. I wondered briefly what had made the brush move in the first place seein' as how the opossum was quite dead, but I declined to poke about in the ditch any further.

By this time, the snake had come up missing, so after finishing a thorough postmortem examination of the opossum, I climbed out of the ditch and mounted up. As I started back down the road, I was musing to myself about finding the odd-looking critter. The term playing possum came to mind. He sure did look dead, I thought. He did look bad: the tongue hanging out, the lifeless stare, the smell. I began turning it over in my head. What made those reeds move? He sure looked to me like he had been dead awhile. Was there anoth-

er animal down in the ditch? I stopped the bike and looked back over my shoulder.

Playin' possum... I had only traveled several hundred feet or so. I wheeled the bike around and coasted up to the clump of reeds.

There was barely a blade of grass bent over where the opossum had lain.

I slowly criss-crossed the section of ditch, then clambered up the far side and searched the edge of the brush. It was gone. For a split second I began to doubt that I had ever seen it in the first place. But the stick I had used to poke the lifeless carcass with was lying right where I'd dropped it.

After some careful thought and a little research at the library, I came to the conclusion that the opossum must have been down in the ditch hunting or feeding on something when I stepped down into it looking for the snake. Startled, the marsupial initiated the behavior for which it had become famous. Once I left, it merely got back on its feet and waddled on its merry way, leaving me temporarily perplexed and more than a little impressed.

Natural History

The Virginia opossum grows to about the size of your average house cat. Coloration is usually a variation of grizzled white above, with long white hairs covering black-tipped fur below. In some areas, individuals may appear grayish or blackish. They sport a long, naked prehensile tail. The head and throat are whitish with large naked ears that are black with pinkish tips. Their legs are short with the first toe of the hind foot opposable (thumb-like) and lacking a claw. Females have a fur-lined abdominal pouch. Opossums measure 25 to 40 inches in length. The tail is 10⅛ to 21 inches long. The hind foot measures 1⅞ to 3⅛ inches. Opossums leave very distinctive looking tracks that are unlike other terrestrial animals. Their weight averages between 4 to14 pounds.

Their reproductive behavior includes a 12- to 13-day gestation, after which 1 to14 young attach themselves to mother's nipples for 2 months. There can be two or three litters per year.

Opossum habitat can be deciduous forests, open woods, brushy wastelands, and farmlands.

Their range covers most of the eastern United States, except northern Minnesota, northern Michigan, and northern New England. It extends southwest to eastern Wyoming, Colorado, and central New Mexico. It also includes southern British Columbia, south to Baja California and east into central Idaho and southeast Arizona.

A solitary nocturnal animal, the Virginia opossum is terrestrial and arboreal, and climbs well. Although it does not hibernate, during very cold weather it may hole up for several days at a time, risking frostbite on its naked ears and tail to seek food when hunger strikes. Carrion forms much of its diet, and many individuals are killed on highways while attempting to feed on road kill. The diet also includes insects, frogs, birds, snakes, small mammals, earthworms, berries, and other fruit; persimmons, apples, and corn are favorite foods. Opossums engage in scent marking, especially during the breeding season, by licking themselves and rubbing the sides of their heads against tree trunks or other objects. Because the penis is forked, there is a myth that this species mates through the female's nose. The Virginia opossum makes a leaf nest in a hollow log, fallen tree, abandoned burrow, or other sheltered place. After a gestation of less than 2 weeks, the living embryos, each the size of a navy bean, climb up through the hair of the female and enter the vertical opening of her pouch. Each takes 1 of her 13 nipples in its mouth and remains thus attached to the mother for 2 months. Those who do not obtain a nipple perish. Several defensive behaviors have been described in opossums. When threatened, an individual may roll over, shut its eyes, and allow its tongue to loll, feigning death, or playing possum, for some time. More often, it tries to bluff its attacker by hissing, screeching, salivating, opening its mouth wide to show all 50 of its teeth, and sometimes excreting a greenish substance. Many of these behaviors occur in encounters between males. Clicks, used in aggressive displays by males during mating season, are also employed in communications between mother and young.

Urban Opossums

This is another creature that folks are astounded by when they discover it in their neighborhood. And since North America's only marsupial acts totally different from most animals, it is common for people to insist that (a) it is sick, (b) it doesn't belong there, or (c) it is dangerous. Most of the time, they're wrong on all counts. Being a marsupial, one of its physiological traits is a somewhat lower body temperature. This actually makes it highly resistant to many pathogens, among them the rabies virus. They are slow-moving, methodical creatures whose savage demeanor, with their mouth agape and drooling, has to be a huge part of their natural defenses.

Opossums love to scavenge in suburbia. Improperly contained trash, excess bird seed, and pet food left outside draw opossums like a magnet. Opossums are nomadic, and they will move through urban environs temporarily denning wherever they can and eating largely what we provide for them. I think most of us would be astounded at how much road kill opossums consume. Between that and their penchant for feeding on rodents, I consider them one of the most beneficial animals in the environment.

Opossums have a knack for getting stuck in garbage cans. They can get in them quite easily and for obvious reasons, but once inside, they become prisoners of our smooth sided refuse containers, unable to climb back out. Any opossum still on its feet that is found in a garbage can, can often be safely released by merely laying the can down on its side and walking away. The opossum will sooner or later wander out of the can and be on its way. Be patient. It found its way into the can because it was hungry, not because it was sick.

Porcupines can be described as large, armored rodents with a chunky body, high-arching back, and short legs. They have long guard hairs on the front half of the body. Overall coloration is black or brown in the East, and more yellowish in the West. Porcupines have quills on the rump and tail. Their feet have unique soles with small, pebbly textured fleshy knobs and long, curved claws with four toes on the front feet and five toes on the back. Porcupines can get quite large, up to 3 feet or more in length, and can weigh 40 pounds.

Porcupines may lash out with their spiny tails if approached too closely. Contrary to popular myth, porkies cannot shoot their quills out. The quills can however, become painfully embedded in the victim's skin. Cutting the end off the quill's base releases air pressure, allowing it to be pulled out more easily.

Breeding occurs from October through November, with one young born sometime in May or June after a gestation period of about 7 months.

They inhabit deciduous, coniferous, and mixed forests in the East, and in the West they can be found in dry, scrubby areas with scattered trees. Range includes most of Canada and the western United States south to eastern Mexico, south to Wisconsin, most of Michigan, and most of Pennsylvania, New York, and New England.

The solitary porcupine is active year-round, but in severe cold it may den up in rocky terrain, sometimes with others of its species. Primarily nocturnal, it may also rest by day in a tree cavity or log, underground burrow, or treetop. It is an excellent climber, yet the animal can occasionally fall.

On the ground, it has an unhurried, waddling walk, relying on its quills for protection from predators. Porcupines usually prefer to walk away or climb a tree rather than confront an enemy. Long claws assist them in climbing, helping them hold on to crevices in bark. The stiff, backward-pointing quills of the underside of the tail help keep them from slipping back down a tree.

The common porcupine has up to 30,000 quills on its body; these are modified hairs, solid at tip and base, hollow for most of the shaft, and loosely attached to a sheet of voluntary muscles beneath the skin. The loosely attached quills detach easily and are driven forcefully into the victim, often with the help of some tail lashing. The unlucky victim's body heat causes the microscopic barbs on the end of each quill to expand and become even more firmly embedded. Wounds may become infected. The quill, depending on where it enters, may blind the victim or prevent it from eating. The short tail quills are the most dangerous since they can be driven deeply into the flesh. Fortunately, porcupines are not aggressive and if left alone, they will not attack. A black line runs up the middle of the tail and expands on the lower back, and there is white on the head. This contrasting, black-and-white warning pattern is similar to that of the skunk, apparently communicating to a potential adversary that it should keep its distance. The porcupine often tries to keep the black-and-white warning coloration of its backside toward potential enemies. If feeling strongly threatened, it may give a second warning, tooth-chattering for up to half a minute, which may be repeated several times. In addition, the porcupine can produce a strong, pungent odor, which in confined quarters, such as a porcupine den, can cause the eyes and nose to water. If all else fails, the porcupine erects its quills. There are a few carnivores, one of them being the fisher, that are adept at flipping a porcupine over to attack its unprotected underside, but even a fisher occasionally receives a fatal injury.

A strict vegetarian, the common porcupine feeds on leaves, twigs, and such green plants as skunk cabbage, lupines, and clover. During the wintertime, it chews through the rough outer bark of various trees, including pines, fir, cedar, and hemlock, to get at the inner bark (cambium) on which it then mainly subsists. Like many herbivores, the porcupine has bacteria in its digestive tract containing enzymes that help to digest the cellulose and other substances not sufficiently broken down by normal digestive enzymes.

Porky's have favorite feeding trees that can be recognized by their cropped and stunted upper branches and bare wood. Another unmistakable sign of porcupines, often littering the ground under favorite trees, are niptwigs. These are the terminal branches of trees that have been cut off, and their leaves or buds eaten. In the Catskill Mountains of New York State, porcupines are fond of sugar maples and young beech trees. They also like basswood, apple, aspen, young ash leaves, acorns, and beechnuts when available.

Fond of salt, porcupines have a great appetite for wooden tool handles that have absorbed human perspiration through use. The animal may kill trees by stripping away the bark, and its gnawing may damage buildings and furniture. The life span of the common porcupine is 7 to 8 years. In addition to the fisher, predators include the mountain lion, bobcat, and coyote. Porcupine quills, both natural and dyed, are used in brilliantly executed decorative quillwork by Native Americans, who also eat the animal's flesh.

Chewing by porcupines can sometimes be eliminated by a variety of metal barriers. Hardware cloth can be wrapped around trees in much the same fashion as it is used to prevent damage by beavers, keeping in mind that the porcupine can climb. Porcupines that are chewing on buildings can often be thwarted by nailing on a strip of metal flashing. Oddly enough, porcupines can be attracted to the glue used in various types of wood construction such as plywood. With this fact in mind, homeowners choosing to build or resurface homes, sheds, and cottages in porcupine country would do well to choose vinyl or aluminum siding, which does not seem to interest porcupines as much.

Chapter 19 - **Rabbit Trails**

The little creek does a lot of meandering on its way to Lake Ontario. During its journey, it travels through one of the many small farms common to the area. There are some wood lots, apple orchards, and also some fields of corn and soybeans. Before and after the deer season, I can pretty much have this place to myself. I go there often to fly my red-tailed hawks. It's not so much that I'm being secretive, but it's nice, when practicing an art like falconry, to not have any more distractions than necessary.

When I started learning this ancient art, I was urged to hunt rabbits. I was taught that it built a solid relationship between you and the hawk. This worked well for us, I guess, when we could find bunnies. Yet, one of the more annoying facts about rabbits is that they only seem to be where you find them! Seriously, rabbit populations tend to be cyclical in nature. For a couple seasons, it seems as though everywhere you step, a cottontail comes bouncing out. Then, all of a sudden, nobody's home. It can really be boom or bust. There are multiple reasons for this, and much of it is related to habitat and weather. Severe wet weather can increase mortality for cottontails. Diseases and parasitism can have their effects as well. The factors that limit rabbits remain largely unseen by most of us. Those of us involved in wildlife rehabilitation often get insights into it by virtue of the number of animals treated and how often the phone rings. A few days of sudden wet weather and large amounts of rainfall can flood out many cottontail nests. If these conditions persist, rabbit numbers can go down in those areas.

Fortunately, rabbits reproduce... well, like rabbits! They can bounce back relatively quickly depending on how much pressure they are under. The fact is rabbits are just about one notch above grass on the food chain. The average lifespan of many cottontail rabbits is only about 9 months.

One day in late winter, I was poking through the winding creek bottom looking for rabbits. After watching me for a minute, Kira, my red-tailed hawk, flew ahead of me and perched in a big willow overlooking the widest part of the creek bottom. We had done this kind of thing before, and she knew what I was up to. We flushed a couple bunnies from their thick hiding places, but for one reason or another, despite her awesome flying and determination, the hawk kept coming up empty. Hunting with a trained raptor can be fascinating, but if I had to hunt to put food on the table, I would pick another way to hunt rabbits.

I noticed that gradually, in the few inches of snow down in the creek bottom, I began to see other types of tracks mixed in with the rabbit sign. I soon recognized them as coyote tracks. There were lots of them. I remember thinking to myself how it had been awhile since I had seen that many predator tracks along with that many rabbit tracks all in the same place.

I smiled to myself thinking of how, when the conversation turns to rabbits, many usually end up blaming the foxes and coyotes for eating all the rabbits. Now, nobody knows better than me that it doesn't take many bunnies to make an awful lot of tracks. But I also know what wildlife biologists have known for years, and that is you can't have predators without having prey. It will always be a self-limiting thing. We see what we want to see and often make assumptions without all the information. I know one thing for sure: if I think too much about food webs, population dynamics, predator/prey relationships, and all that stuff, it starts to take all the fun and mystery out of it all. I try to leave nothing behind in the woods except my tracks and let God take care of the rest of it.

Cottontail Facts

The familiar cottontail of the eastern United States is usually a grayish brown above, grizzled with black, with the forehead often having a white spot. They can also show a distinct rust colored nape. The tail is cottony white below. The feet are whitish above. The ears are long.

A similar species is represented by the New England cottontail. This species usually lacks the rust-colored nape and has a black patch between the ears. The desert cottontail is usually smaller, with slightly longer ears. Marsh and swamp rabbits have rust-colored feet. Snowshoe hares are usually larger and uniform dark brown in summer.

Breeding can take place from February through September. Gestation is 28 to 32 days. Rabbits usually have three or four litters per year, each consisting of one to nine young (usually four or five).

Cottontails inhabit brushy areas, old fields, woods, and cultivated areas, especially around thickets and brush piles. They range throughout the eastern United States, except for New England, and west through North Dakota, Kansas, and Texas. They are also found in New Mexico and Arizona.

The most common rabbit in much of the United States, the eastern cottontail is primarily nocturnal, but is active near dawn and dusk, and often on dark days. Cottontails usually hop, but they can leap 10 to 15 feet. They sometimes stand on their hind feet to view their surroundings. When pursued, they usually circle their territory and often jump sideways to break their scent trail. They dislike getting wet but will swim if pressed. In winter, when brush is strong enough to hold a covering blanket of snow, they often make a network of runways beneath it. In cold weather, they often use woodchuck burrows.

This species feeds on many different plants, mainly herbaceous varieties in summer and woody varieties in winter. As is the case with many lagomorphs, in addition to producing typical fecal pellets, the eastern cottontail will feed rapidly, then retreat to the safety of a brush pile or other shelter and defecate soft green pellets, or night stools, which are eaten later to further the process of digestion. Rabbits mastered the idea of recycling long before us humans.

During the breeding season, males fight one another and perform dance-like courtship displays for the territorial females. These displays involve face-offs and much jumping, including females jumping over males. Individuals often jump straight up into the air, and pairs or small groups often engage in active chases. The young are born in a nest lined with plant material and fur from the mother's breast. The nest cavity, in a hollow in the ground, is about 7 inches deep and 5 inches wide. The top of the nest is covered over with vegetation. It is common for nests in lawns to be exposed when lawn mowers take the tops off. The young are nursed at dawn and dusk. Within hours after giving birth, the female mates again. If no young are lost, a single pair, together with their offspring, could produce 350,000 rabbits in 5 years. However, this rabbit's death rate vies with its birth rate, with few individuals living longer than one year.

Rabbits that insist on munching in the garden can be repelled with a mixture called Bunny Stay-Away, which can be made in the kitchen for a few pennies, or with a couple of commercial repellents available from your local nursery.

BUNNY STAY-AWAY

1 whole Spanish onion

1 jalapeño pepper

1 Tbsp. cayenne pepper

Chop onion and jalapeño pepper. Mix together with cayenne pepper and boil in 2 qts. water. Let boil 20 minutes. Let cool. Strain water through cheesecloth into container (straining is VERY IMPORTANT—even small chunks of the vegetables will clog spray bottles). Put Bunny Stay-Away in a squirt bottle or garden sprayer and spray all affected areas. Spray daily for 2 weeks, and then repeat spray weekly and after rain. This mixture is non-toxic to bunnies and other animals. It is safe for plants and vegetables. **REMEMBER: The key to this recipe is the APPLICATION. You need to spray affected areas EVERY DAY for TWO FULL WEEKS to break bunny's habit of munching in that location.** After that, just touch up your spraying once a week, but be sure to re-spray after every rainfall.

Consider the use of repellants in conjunction with low fencing where applicable. In any nuisance animal situation, it is often the combination of several methods that can give the maximum benefit.

These days, tree climbing seems to be yet another lost art. I can't remember the last time I saw a kid climbing a tree. For us, climbing a tree meant you had a power and control over the world that no one else possessed. To be able to magically change your whole perspective at will was heady stuff for a kid. We had our favorites. The tall elm in the neighbor's front yard, the willows in our backyard, or the silver maples that stood like soldiers between the two properties. When a new tree was discovered—one that hadn't been climbed before— you immediately had to make an attempt. After all, it was a matter of personal honor.

It wasn't like we didn't know about the old crab apple tree. Its branches reached above the hedgerow that it stood in the center of. But the hedgerow was thick, and there were trees that were much easier to approach. That was, until my dad had the occasion to clear some brush in the hedge creating a path to the tree.

The old gnarled apple tree had a big hole in it right at the base of the Y it formed about 15 feet up. This feature made it all the more irresistible. There could be long-forgotten treasure in that hole, stashed there by pirates or bank robbers. I mean, anything could be in that hole.

I started up. It was a tough one—not many low branches—but I eventually gained a foothold and made my way up the tree. In order to stick my face in that hole, I had to stand spread eagle with one foot way out to the left, and the other way out to right. That's why in those days any tree-climbing kid worth his salt climbed barefoot.

Reaching up with my right hand, I grabbed hold of a big knot sticking out of the side of the trunk, pulled myself up to eye level with the hole, and peered into the blackness. It took a couple of seconds for my eyes to adjust to the dark interior of the tree cavity, and another second or two for my mind to process what I was seeing.

Inches from my face was another face: a furry face with pointed nose and characteristic black mask. The raccoon never moved and never made a sound. It stared back at me as if waiting for me to make the first move. I have forgotten my exact age at that time, but I was no more than 10 or 11 years old. By this time in my young life, following my elders around in the woods on hunting trips had taught me to freeze when wildlife was sighted. There was no place I could get to quick anyway, so we stared each other down for what seemed like an eternity. Slowly, I lowered my face away and out of view of the hole and desperately looked down to change my foothold. Needless to say, when I got low enough I took the express exit out of the tree. The raccoon never made a noise, never followed me, and never even stuck its head out of the hole. To this day, I have never come upon an adult raccoon in a cavity or dwelling that didn't just freeze and wait for the human to decide how to handle the situation.

Bandits in the Nights

The raccoon (Procyon lotor) is intelligent, powerful, and possesses a dexterity in its front limbs approaching that of a primate. It can easily be identified by the prominent black mask and ringed tail. Its size can vary quite a bit, anywhere from 10 to 30 pounds in weight. It can be a common night visitor to your trash cans and if successful, will put you on its regular route. Raccoons love to explore people's attics or garages in search of an alternate denning site. The female will have her cubs there, and the male, or boar, will alternate his den site every couple of nights during mild weather. This explains why people who discover they have a nuisance raccoon on their property sometimes don't hear or see it every night.

The raccoon is a very successful urban resident that feeds on a wide variety of plant and animal materials. Omnivorous, the raccoon feeds on wild fruits, grapes, berries, fish, shellfish, crustaceans, grubs, crickets, grasshoppers, mice and other small mammals, bird eggs, and nestlings. Upon reading this partial list of foods, it is not hard to see why the raccoon has such an interest in our eating habits, and why they are often found hanging around our garbage cans and dumpsters. Raccoons are very active at night, and although considered mostly nocturnal, it is not all that unusual to see one moving about during the daylight hours, depending on the time of year.

Many people love to feed raccoons. This is not advisable as raccoons can quickly become too comfortable around humans, creating the potential for problems. In much of the eastern part of the United States, the raccoon is listed as a rabies vector species. This classification sounds ominous, but really just means that this particular species is proving to be a reservoir for the rabies virus, providing a means for the disease to spread among a population. It does not mean that every individual of that species is carrying the virus. What it means, from a practical standpoint, is that everyone should use a little caution and a lot of common sense when confronted with all forms of wildlife in general, and those animals deemed rabies vector species in particular.

Raccoons are just one of the cavity-dwelling species of animals that are known for exploiting habitat and becoming unwelcome guests on our property. Female raccoons that have chosen the attic, eaves, or shed to have their babies in can often be evicted rather easily. We need to remember that the raccoon has chosen that place because it felt it was a safe, dark place (like a hole in a tree). The first course of action should be to modify the environment so that it is just the opposite. Illumination with an extension cord and work light, plus the addition of a radio or boom box is my personal first choice. The more obnoxious the choice of music, the better. Change that dark quiet hideaway into a swingin' nightclub, and 80 to 90 percent of the time, mom will move the kids within 12 hours. Like most cavity dwellers, she already has an alternate den site in mind, so she just has to decide that it's time to move. Babies found with no adult can often mean mom is away hunting. Open the nightclub anyway, and when mom gets back she will often decide the jig is up and it's time to go. A word of caution is necessary here: Very young raccoons are unbelievably cute. If discovered out of the den or exposed by some means, they should never be handled. Direct human contact with rabies vector species, no matter how young they are, becomes a matter of public health and can often result in the need to destroy the young in order to test them for rabies. If baby raccoons are discovered, contact a wildlife rehabilitator first before touching them.

Raccoons are also big on garbage cans. They are good at it too. The bigger and more experienced the coon, the more persistent it can be. Trash receptacles of large, sturdy design and fastened to the side of the building or in their own cart are a good idea. Likewise, not putting them out until pick-up day is a great idea if they can be kept in a secure shed or garage.

Raccoons that have learned to pull the lids off trash cans can be thwarted by using a bungee cord to fasten the lid on, or by simply putting a brick on top. Remember that in order to pull off the lid, the coon usually has to tip over the can first. If the can is in a cart or fastened upright, the coon may climb up on top but then often can't pull the lid off because it's sitting on the can.

Feeding pets or wildlife off the back porch is never a good idea, and raccoons are just one of the reasons. Many people who think they are doing the neighborhood stray cat population a good deed are often unwittingly feeding raccoons that are all too happy to cruise the neighborhood after dark and hit every porch they can before the cats get there.

Another habit of raccoons that seems to drive some people nuts is sleeping out in the open, up in the crotch of a tree. I have witnessed this behavior in suburban and woodland raccoons many times. Many people seeing it for the first time just can't believe that the coon isn't either trapped (I love that one) or sick. The irony, for me, is that most of us as a species love to lounge around on a nice sunny day, doing as little as possible, and hate to be bothered while doing it.

For the sake of this chapter we will consider rodents as mice, house mice, rats, wood rats, Norway rats, etc. Any rodent found commonly living near or among humans. This chapter isn't aimed so much at natural history as it is at behavior. If you're thinking rodent behavior, you're only part right. Human behavior is at least half the problem—most of the time.

The cosmos are in alignment for most species of rodents that choose to live among us. Life has never been better. Although I hesitate to speak in generalities, let me say that we humans are, by and large, a lazy bunch. Messy too. We often wait too long to put the trash out. When we do, a lot of the time it's just in a garbage bag. We love to have firewood available for those cold nights in front of the fire but never seem to use as much of it as we think. Or perhaps the woodstove or fireplace falls into disrepair, and so, the wood just sits there, often in a messy pile. Those of us that run businesses, especially restaurants, wait until the very last minute to call for a dumpster pick-up. Old cars, broken patio furniture, cardboard boxes, and debris of all kinds litter our properties. We like to feed the birds but are too lazy to buy and maintain a bird feeder, so we just scatter some seed on the ground.

Got some heavy weed growth or tall grass within a hundred feet or so of any of these scenarios? Awesome Rodent Motel. Rodents check in and never check out. They just breed. With all the cover we provide them, it's all the harder for the natural predators of rodents to try to help. We then just start complaining about the fox, skunk, opossum, or coyote that would be more than happy to help us out in keeping rodent populations in check. We yell at the landlord about the mouse or rat problem, but if we're lucky enough to see a fox on patrol nearby, we can't get to the phone or the gun rack fast enough. Nature is waiting to give us a hand if we'll just stop and think.

Several times in this book I have mentioned the term habitat modification. At no time is this concept more important than when dealing with rodent infestations.

I will bet you lunch (and if we've ever met, you know how I feel about lunch) that if you have an actual rodent problem, it is a direct result of something you or your neighbors are either doing or not doing. How close is the nearest fast food establishment, pizzeria, or other commercial business? What are their refuse pick-up policies? How stringent is the municipality that you live in with regard to health code and sanitation enforcement?

As with all nuisance wildlife scenarios, there is rarely just one simple factor involved. Small rodents, like all wild creatures, are uniquely designed to take advantage of food and cover wherever they may be. As always, a thoughtful approach and a comprehensive plan will, more often than not, set the stage for a reduction in animal activity, often without the use of hazardous poisons, baits or haphazard attempts at predator control.

May 1999

It is early morning in the woods. Identifying songbird calls is not my strong suit. But I sometimes like to try. Wood thrush, blue jay (an easy one), and some kind of warbler, I think to myself. A wild turkey gobbles behind me, and as I look over my shoulder, I catch a glimpse of white moving on the forest floor. Like the white rabbit from the Lewis Carroll story, the striped skunk moves right along as if late for an important appointment. Skunks' black-and-white coloration always looks so striking to me, whatever backdrop I see them up against.

I was curious. The skunk was statistically out a little late for a creature that is largely nocturnal, but then again it's risky to speak in absolutes regarding wildlife. I followed its progress as it passed behind my location. To my knowledge, it never detected my presence. Skunks don't have particularly good long-range eyesight. Big, bushy tail flapping; it headed straight for a large, old maple tree. Upon reaching the spreading roots at the base of the tree, the skunk suddenly popped out of sight.

I correctly assumed it had a burrow at the base of the tree. It was a small entrance hole and well protected by the large root system of the maple. I remember thinking to myself that with skunks being so common everywhere else these days, it was almost weird to see a wild skunk out in the woods.

August 2006

The graduation party had dwindled down to just a handful of us sitting around the backyard campfire pit, enjoying the night air and each other's company. We finally said our goodnights and loaded up the car. As we began to drive away down the narrow South Buffalo street, we caught some movement in the headlights. I was about to say "cat," but by then we were close enough to see the unmistakable undulating gait that the whole weasel family is famous for. The skunk lost no time in crossing the street in front of us but paused to look back just before popping under a fence. I smiled to myself and thought "another skunk in its natural habitat."

There's No Place like Home

Maybe it's me, but I sometimes see irony in the strangest circumstances. Take skunks for instance. I can't think of an animal more maligned or subject to human prejudice. Practically no one has anything nice to say about skunks—especially when they find themselves in close proximity to one. And yet skunks will live anywhere. They don't discriminate. I have found skunks in the richest and the poorest of neighborhoods. Anywhere man provides the necessary forms of cover and food, you can bet somewhere you will find a skunk. Skunks, like other burrowing cavity dwellers, are looking for a safe place to dig a burrow or expand an existing one. The rural skunk will use the base of a mature tree, a hedgerow, creek bank, or dead log as protection to guard, hide, and fortify the burrow entrance. The urban skunk finds these types of features in short supply and so, adapts by using sheds, porches, decks, garages, or old woodpiles under which to set up shop.

Many people would be surprised if they knew just how long they were living near skunks before something went wrong, and they found out. There are legitimate instances when skunks just end up in the wrong locale. Under a crawl space, for example, or a burrow that is right outside a basement wall. This makes it tough to live with them for sure, but it is by no means the norm. Lots of folks have skunks on their property right now (finish this chapter before you go run and look) and are unaware of it. This is because skunks only engage in that well-known stinky behavior as a direct response to a threat. Really, you have to literally make contact with or badly scare a skunk before it will spray. I remind people that with the sheer numbers of skunks in urban North America, if they were walking around with the hair trigger people think they have, life on planet earth would stink! (Sorry, couldn't help myself.)

Largely nocturnal, this unassuming omnivore wants nothing to do with us and is happy to leave us alone if we can find it possible to do the same. Where things often go awry in the relationship is with the family dog. Many dogs just can't help themselves. As if in deference to some unwritten code of dog conduct, when the family pooch detects a skunk they immediately go looking for trouble. And when they often find it, then nobody's happy, be it dog, human, or skunk. Another cause of skunk spray is attack by natural predators. The skunk has only one major natural predator: the great horned owl. Like the skunk, the great horned is nocturnal, or crepuscular, and, like most birds, has no sense of smell. Indeed, just about every other horned owl I treat as a wildlife rehabilitator has the faint, familiar aura of skunk about it, or they just downright reek. This large winged predator is common in many areas and thinks nothing of hunting the suburbs at night. It is often the reason for a sudden strong odor of skunk on a midsummer night with no other trace of skunk activity in the immediate area.

It is difficult, once someone has discovered a skunk on their property, to talk about how beneficial these animals are to the environment. The sheer mental hazard of it all often gets in the way. An omnivore, the skunk is very fond of mice, and since many suburbs these days are experiencing rodent problems, the skunks are only too glad to try and help us out. Earthworms, insects, various forms of vegetation, etc., are all on the skunks' menu. Skunks are also fond of digging for grubs in the yard. They have this ability to sense the presence of the grub underground. They dig up a clump of dirt and eat the grub living in the roots. They then toss the tiny divot aside and look for another. If it appears like there may have been drunk leprechauns playing golf on your lawn, it is most likely skunks that have been grubbing. Treating the lawn for grubs often abates this behavior. Other food items are on the skunks' list too. Pet food left outside, excessive birdseed waste under the bird feeder, improperly stored garbage—these are all magnets that attract skunks and other nighttime wildlife.

It is infinitely easier to deny skunks and other species access to certain areas before they take up residence. Sadly, this is not usually the case. If you discover that you have a skunk living on your property, consider a few things first. Where is the skunk's burrow? Is there any actual chronic odor in the home? Do you have a dog, and if so, are the odds very high that the dog and skunk will ever meet? Let's face it, the type of dog can factor in heavily here. A couch potato bulldog or many of the giant breeds couldn't care less. On the other hand, a terrier or sporting breed might be hard pressed to ignore its genetics. (Border collies should just be given written protocols or bribed with the car keys.) Seriously though, try and decide if, or how much, of an actual inconvenience this is liable to be.

If there are no odor problems and the skunk is simply living on the property or moving through, it may have been there for some time. If you detect a burrow and are unsure of whether or not it is a skunk, cross a couple small sticks over the burrow entrance at dusk and then check first thing in the morning. This will help you discern whether there is nocturnal activity at the den site or not. Consider also that as the spring and summer progress into fall and early winter, nature's process of natural attrition reduces the number of skunks in a population and that often means the one living under your pool cabana. The stick trick can come in useful again here and can help you tell if a burrow is still active.

Inactive burrows should be dealt with immediately, if not sooner. If the burrow is under a shed or outbuilding, the use of galvanized mesh, or hardware cloth, works great. Nail or staple it around the perimeter of the structure and have it extend down into the ground at least 6 to 8 inches. This method permanently denies any animal future access to this space. The same method can be used for decks or porches.

There are those times when a skunk will have to be removed in conjunction with repairs and exclusion work. We talked about that in the section entitled "*Nuisance Wildlife.*"

In some parts of the country, skunks are listed as rabies vector species by fish and game departments. This does not mean that every individual of the species has rabies. It means that the virus is commonly found in this species and people should observe caution when handling skunks and their young. A word of caution is necessary here: Very young skunks are unbelievably cute. If discovered out of the den or exposed by some means, they should never be handled. Direct human contact with rabies vector species, no matter how young they are, becomes a matter of public health and can often result in the need to destroy the young in order to test them for rabies. If baby skunks are discovered, as with raccoons, contact a wildlife rehabilitator first before touching them.

Some Natural History

Typically, the striped skunk's color is some variation of black with two broad, white stripes on the back meeting in a cape on the head and shoulders. They often have a thin white stripe down the center of the face. The tail is a bushy black, often with white tip or fringe. Individual coloration varies from mostly black to mostly white. Males are larger than females. Length is 20 to 31 inches. Tails are 7¼ to15½ inches long. Body weight averages 6 to 14 pounds. Other species of skunks include the common hog-nosed skunk, which has a white back and tail, a snout that is naked on top, and no white facial stripe; and the hooded skunk, identified by its longer tail and mostly black coloration with narrow white stripes (in white-backed phase, black hairs are interspersed).

Skunk breeding season is February to April. Total gestation is 62 to 66 days. Litters of four to seven young are born in mid-May; young are blind at birth, and their very fine hair is clearly marked with a black-and-white pattern.

Skunk habitat is everywhere from desert to woodlands, grassy plains, and suburbs. Their range encompasses most of the United States and the southern tier of the Canadian provinces.

Most mammals have coloration that blends with their environment. But the striped skunk, like other skunks, is boldly colored, advertising to potential enemies that it is not to be bothered. Its anal glands hold about a tablespoon of a fetid, oily, yellowish musk, enough for five or six jets of spray—although one is usually enough. When threatened, the striped skunk will face the intruder, arch and elevate its tail, erect the tail hairs, chatter its teeth, and stomp the ground with the front feet. This usually causes the intruder to retreat, but if it remains, the skunk will twist its back around, raise its tail straight up, evert its anal nipples, and spray scent 10 to 15 feet (3 to 5 meters). The mist may reach three times as far, and the smell may carry a mile. Spray in the eyes causes intense pain and fleeting loss of vision.

The striped skunk is primarily nocturnal and does not hibernate, although during extremely cold weather it may become temporarily dormant. The animal's temperature drops only from about 98.6 to 87.8 degrees Fahrenheit (37 to 31 degrees Celsius), rather than down to the temperature of its den.

The striped skunk is an omnivore, feeding heavily on a wide variety of animal food in spring and summer, including insects and grubs, small mammals, the eggs of ground-nesting birds, and amphibians. Some of the more important invertebrate foods consumed are beetles and their larvae, grasshoppers, crickets, earthworms, butterfly and moth larvae, spiders, snails, ants, bees, wasps, and crayfish. This skunk eats fruits in season such as wild cherries, ground cherries, blackberries, blueberries, and many others. In the fall, the animal gorges itself to fatten up in preparation for the lean winter months.

Getting Rid of the Odor...

The material produced in the glands of a skunk is an amazing compound. So much so that it is still used in the making of perfumes because of its natural tenacity. When pets, people, or property have been "skunked," it is time to think about breaking the substance down rather than covering it up. The old standby of tomato juice is not high up on my list. Any real effect this has on skunk odor would be by virtue of the natural acidity in tomato juice. Other than that, you're just covering things up and postponing the agony. There are an abundance of commercially available products for removing skunk odor, and some of them can work pretty well. The best ones are oxidizers that break the skunk odor down chemically. One of the best ones can be made up in the kitchen. Use the recipe below and increase the ratios depending on how much you need.

1 quart hydrogen peroxide

1 quarter cup of baking soda

1 tablespoon of dish detergent preferably Dawn®

Mix these ingredients together and put them in a spray bottle. This mixture has a short shelf life so use it right away. It is safe for pets and most colorfast surfaces though it may temporarily bleach some pet hair. You should test it on anything else if you are uncertain.

Chapter 23 - **A Snake In The Grass**

Common Garter Snake

One way people form attitudes about animals is by what they know, or what they think they know. Another way they form an opinion is by the way an animal makes them feel. By and large, people respond more favorably to animals that they think are attractive, or cute and cuddly. It's probably safe to say that many folks do not think that snakes are particularly attractive. This fact alone can cause these reptiles serious public relations problems in and around our property.

Snakes are one of those animals that evoke strong reactions in people. Whether positive or negative, just the mention of snakes will tell you right away where most folks stand. My mother was born on a small farm along the banks of the Cattaraugus Creek in the southern tier of New York State. Her mother, my grandmother, told me that a number of times she had seen a snake grab itself by the tail and roll down a hill like a hoop. Being somewhat interested in snakes at that time, I tried to tell her, as diplomatically as a teenager could, that this was not physically possible. It was the only time I can remember my grandmother becoming upset with me.

Strangely enough, even those of us who appreciate snakes and are thankful for how beneficial they are to the environment, are often momentarily startled when we come upon one. The good news is that in North America non-venomous species far outnumber their venomous counterparts. Indeed, even in those areas of the country where venomous species are common, you're much more likely to run into harmless species. All across North America, we have what biologists refer to as *colubrid* snakes, or any one of a number of species of smooth-scaled, non-venomous snakes, which include king snakes, rat snakes, garter snakes, and water snakes.

Identifying venomous and non-venomous snakes can usually be done by comparing the shape of the head. In North America, all but one venomous species belong to the family of pit vipers. The heads of all vipers are characteristically broad, flat, and somewhat triangular in shape, while the previously mentioned colubrids have a distinctly narrow head that is often smaller than their overall body diameter. The rare exception to this rule would be the diminutive and secretive coral snake of the extreme southeastern United States. In addition, the scales of vipers have a central ridge, or keel, while most non-venomous snakes are smooth scaled.

All snakes share the same trait in that they are *poikilothermic*, or cold-blooded. They, like all other reptiles, depend on their surroundings for controlling their body temperature. Most snakes in North America are fond of basking, or soaking up the sun's warmth in order to raise their metabolic rate. This sometimes explains why they end up under foot, so to speak. Since they do not have external ears, snakes are incredibly sensitive to vibrations and thus are usually moving out of our way long before we see them.

A person finding snakes on their property often correlates with the seasons because of the tendency for snakes to congregate just before and after their winter hibernation. Many species of snakes use the same den, or hibernacula, every year. This winter refuge can be nothing more than a hole or crack in the ground leading to a cavity below or near the frost line. Rock piles, stone or concrete patios, bridge abutments, and old foundations can either serve as, or guard, the entrance to a hibernation den.

All snakes play a beneficial role in the environment. They consume huge amounts of insects and great numbers of rodents. Most problems associated with snakes have to do with our own individual perception of snakes, and not with any actual damage or threat from the snake. There are instances when snakes find their way into our homes. Once again, it is investigation and repair or modification that will ultimately make everyone happy.

Snakes blunder into buildings for two reasons, and two reasons only. Either the snakes are trying to escape heat or cold through cracks or crevices in building foundations, or they are sensing the presence of food within the confines of the building. Count on the fact that any snake can pour itself through an opening less than half of its body diameter.

One of the best products that homeowners can invest in to stop many kinds of unwanted entry is the kind of expandable polyurethane foam used to insulate around window and door frames after installation. Marketed under a couple different brand names, it comes in an aerosol container with a detachable tube that can be inserted into all manner of cracks, voids, and crevices. A simple push of the button injects a small amount of foam into the crack where it expands to several times its original size, effectively sealing the opening against any further entry. This method, coupled with the removal of any rodent or insect infestation, usually mitigates any kind of snake activity.

How'd He Do That, Houdini?

Snakes are masters of escape. An "escape-proof" snake enclosure is just one that the snake hasn't figured out yet. Let's face it: the snake has nothing but time on its hands.

A large part of my youth was spent catching, keeping, and studying snakes. I mentioned before that I was lucky enough to have really patient parents. Periodically, for one reason or another, I sometimes found myself pushing the envelope of their good nature when it came to my animal mania.

My black rat snake wasn't exactly the cuddliest representative of his genus. He was almost 6 feet in length, and when provoked (just looking at him often did the trick), he had this habit of rearing a good 2½ feet of his length off the ground and hissing at you like some badass, venomous wannabe. At the time, I thought it was pretty cool. But I guess if you didn't know him, he could be a little intimidating.

I wish I could say that for all the years I collected snakes I never had any escape, but that would be a really big fib. I came home one day, and the big rat snake had somehow gotten out. Over the years, I had adopted a strict nondisclosure policy toward making any upsetting announcements about snakes loose in the house. Rather, I would nonchalantly as possible begin inspecting every nook, cranny, and crevice in ever-widening circles from the point of origin. This usually worked for the FBI, so I was constantly adapting the technique to my own use. If caught, I could always sing like a ca-

nary, but until then I kept my mouth shut and stayed on the trail.

Johnny Carson was over and everyone in the house was turning in for the night. I can still remember the sound of my parents' bedroom door closing after my mother said good night. I had just crawled into bed and listened as the house became quiet. Suddenly, the sound of my name split the night. Not just my first name, but my middle name too. Being summoned by both names was never a good thing. Along with intense irritation, I sensed a certain level of urgency in my mother's voice.

Upon entering the room, I found my mother in her nightgown standing off to the side and pointing to her open closet door. "Get...him...out of here!" she ordered.

Coiled defensively on the floor of my mother's closet was all 6 feet of rat snake. It was at that moment that I realized I had neglected to bring the snake hook with me. It was more of a luxury than a real necessity, as although the rat snake was non-venomous, when upset, he could draw blood on occasion. My mother could, as all mothers can, read her children's minds and shot me a withering look as I left to retrieve the proper tool. Ultimately the rat snake was returned to its enclosure. Looking back, I'm still not sure who was more ticked off: the big constrictor, or my mom.

Grey Squirrel

Going Nuts

The eastern gray squirrel is a familiar sight scampering across the tree-lined streets of our cities and suburbs. Many people enjoy this frequent visitor to their backyards and bird feeders, and usually its only crimes are not leaving much for the birds and making a mess at the feeder.

Gray squirrels are highly active early and late in the day and will eat a variety of seeds, grains and nuts, either naturally occurring or in feeders. In addition, they will take advantage of certain agricultural crops such as corn and soybeans. When presented with the opportunity, squirrels will also raid bird nests for eggs and nestlings.

The feeding of gray squirrels can become a controversial issue in residential areas because once they become accustomed to visiting an area, they are slow to leave. Sooner or later, they run afoul of someone who is not a squirrel fan. During the course of its travels through the canopy of trees, where it spends a lot of its time, the gray squirrel often finds itself on the roof of someone's home where it continues to explore for potential nesting sites, places to cache food, and areas to escape from predators.

Unfortunately, this normal squirrel behavior sets the stage for the squirrel to take up residence in the attic or get caught in the heating ducts by way of an uncapped chimney. Homeowners can head off this potential problem by inspecting their property for uncapped chimneys, or cracks or separations in the eaves and overhangs of their homes. Any opening large enough for the squirrel to get its face into is a potential entry point. Although capable of defending itself when cornered, we have nothing to fear from these bushy-tailed city dwellers, and they provide us a good excuse to periodically inspect our property before they do.

Squirrels can be one of the easiest animals to get to leave on their own, or what we call self evict. That is, if you can get to them. Squirrels often utilize eaves, soffits, and overhangs as nurseries in which to rear their young. The main point to remember is that squirrels, like most cavity dwellers, usually have a secondary den site waiting in reserve. If at all possible, exposing the den and young will, more often than not, cause the female to immediately set about relocating the young to another den site. This may sometimes mean removing a facia board or soffit panel. Keep in mind that some form of disrepair was responsible for the squirrels being there in the first place, and some level of repair and/or exclusion will be needed anyway. Getting the female squirrel to move the young herself is always the best, most effective, and cheapest way to go in the long run. Squirrel dens that can't be exposed or gotten to in some way may need to be dealt with by licensed wildlife removal personnel.

Squirrel Facts

Gray squirrels are gray above with buff underfur showing especially on the head, shoulders, back, and feet. The underbelly is a paler gray. The flattened tail is bushy gray with silvery-tipped hairs. In Canada and the Northeast, some have reddish, or *rufous*, bellies and tails. The black, or *melanistic*, phase is common in the northern parts of their range. Length is 17 to 19 inches. Tail length is 8¼ to 9⅜ inches. Gray squirrels can weigh 14⅛ to 25 ounces (400 to 710 grams). A similar species called the eastern fox squirrel is larger and has orange or yellow-tipped tail hairs.

Gray squirrels have two litters per year. One litter of two or three young is born in spring, with a second litter born in late summer. Gestation lasts about 44 days. Habitat includes hardwood or mixed forests with nut trees, especially oak-hickory forests. Gray squirrels will also use agricultural crops when available.

The range of the gray covers the eastern United States, east of southern Manitoba, eastern North Dakota, most of Iowa, eastern Kansas, eastern Oklahoma, and eastern Texas. This species has also been introduced to many locations outside of its native range including San Francisco, California and Seattle, Washington.

Especially active in the morning and evening, the eastern gray squirrel is abroad all year, even digging through snow in intense cold to retrieve buried nuts. The only large squirrel in much of the northeastern United States, it feeds especially heavily on hickory nuts, beechnuts, acorns, and walnuts. It does not cache nuts where it finds them but carries them to a new spot, burying each nut individually in a hole dug with the forefeet and then tamped down with the forefeet, hind feet, and nose. Most nuts are buried at the surface, with few more than ¼ inches (6 to 8 millimeters) below the ground. In this fashion, many trees are propagated, although the animal may nip off the germinating end of the nut before burying it, which prevents germination. About 85 percent of the nuts may be recovered. Nuts buried by scientists conducting an experiment were recovered by the squirrels at about the same rate as nuts they buried themselves, indicating that memory is not involved in nut recovery. This squirrel can smell buried nuts under a foot of snow; when snow is deep, the squirrel tunnels under it to get closer to the scent.

Besides nuts, the eastern gray squirrel feeds on a great number of other items as available, including maple buds, bark, samaras, tulip tree blossoms, apples, fungi, and a wide variety of seeds, as well as the occasional insect. They are also known to prey on birds and their nests. These squirrels are ever on the move about their home ranges, so they are always abreast of the many potential food items. They usually feed on just one food at a time, changing the item as additional sources come along. Buried nuts and other items are the mainstays in winter and in spring, but other foods are heavily consumed as they ripen. There is a great increase of activity in fall, when the squirrels spend most of their time cutting and burying nuts. Sometimes there is a rain of nuts on the forest floor, especially when the animals cut white oak acorns.

The eastern gray squirrel dens in trees year-round, using either natural cavities and old woodpecker holes, or leaf nests in stout, mature trees or standing dead ones, especially white oaks, beeches, elms, and red maples. Tree cavities must be at least 12 inches (300 millimeters) deep and have an opening at least 3 inches (75 millimeters) in diameter. Both males and females build winter nests and more loosely constructed summer nests, which are likely to be near dens but are not always in the same trees. Rough population estimates have been made by assuming 1½ leaf nests per squirrel. Leaf nests are difficult to spot in summer because they are made of green leaves, but nests are very obvious in winter. The more permanent nests are woven together well to weather the elements. Extremely ramshackle nests may have been damaged by the elements but are likely to have been built by juveniles, or as temporary shelters near corn or other attractive crops.

The eastern gray squirrel mates in midwinter; a mating "chase" is often involved, with several males following a female as she moves about during the day. Frequently, the spring litter of young is born in a tree cavity, while the second, late-summer litter is born in a leaf nest. Females often move their litters back and forth between cavity dens and leaf nests, perhaps because of changes in the weather, or to escape predation or parasite infestation. The young are weaned in about 50 days. The second litter stays with the female over the winter. The characteristic aggressive bark of the eastern gray squirrel—*que, que, que, que*—is usually accompanied by flicks of the tail. It makes other calls as well, including a loud, nasal cry.

The gray squirrel's tail is used primarily for balance in trees, but serves as a sunshade, an umbrella, a blanket, and a rudder when swimming. It gives lift when the squirrel leaps from branch to branch and slows descent should the squirrel fall. Overpopulation may trigger major migrations of this squirrel species. In the early 19th century, when vast tracts of the East were covered by dense hardwood forest, observers reported migrations in which squirrels never touched ground but moved great distances from tree to tree. A major migration of thousands of squirrels took place in October 1968 in Tennessee, Georgia, and North Carolina. This movement was attributed to substantial nut production and a high reproduction rate in 1967, followed by a late frost and little nut production in 1968. Black and gray phases of this species often are found together, leading some to think they are two different species. There are albino colonies in Olney, Illinois; Trenton, New Jersey;

and Greenwood, South Carolina. There are other species of tree and ground squirrels found throughout the United States. There are many similarities among them that would apply to living with them and abating any nuisance issues.

Eastern Painted Turtle

First, here are some general definitions: A turtle is a shelled reptile that spends all or part of its time in or around water. Many, but not all species have webbed feet. A tortoise is a shelled reptile that does not swim and usually does not live near water, but more often lives in arid or subtropical regions.

Two species of turtles are very common and often seen in and around the suburbs. The first is the eastern or western painted turtle. It is characterized by a smooth, dark green shell, green head with various stripes, and the distinct habit of basking or sunning itself on logs or rocks in or at the water's edge. These turtles are often found in the dangerous act of crossing the highway in search of high and dry ground to dig their nests. This behavior usually begins in late May to early June and continues into early July. *If it can be done safely, caring motorists should move turtles off the road in the direction that they are found traveling.* The urge to breed and lay eggs is strong, and if turned around before they have completed their mission, they will merely attempt to cross again and again. Painted turtles eat a large amount of fish and invertebrates during the early years of their life span, supplementing their diet with plant material as they age.

The next most common species of turtle is the common snapping turtle. This turtle is easily identified by its often large size, large thick tail, and heavy muscular legs. The next most common trait would be its pugnacious attitude when confronted out of water—this helps give the animal its name. The size range for this turtle can vary quite a bit. Some individuals grow up to and in excess of 30 pounds! They can also be very long-lived with documented cases of 75 years or more. Snappers, for the most part, do not bask but live the majority of their lives under water in solitude, waiting for their dinner to swim by. Their diet can consist of any small fish, reptile, amphibian, bird, or mammal that swims too close. However, fish, frogs, and carrion routinely make up the majority of this turtle's diet. Snapping turtles are also in the habit of crossing the roads in search of nest sites, and as a result, often sustain horrible injuries. It should be noted that an adult snapping turtle of even a modest size is capable of inflicting a very painful and possibly dangerous bite. Although totally harmless when in the water, they should be treated with caution when found on land.

Snapping Turtle Natural History

Much of the common literature describes the snapping turtle's size range as 8 to 18½ inches. Indeed, most people encounter this interesting turtle within this size range. However, the familiar snapper, with massive head and powerful jaws, can be found occasionally much larger, and these individuals can be quite old indeed. The upper shell, or carapace, is tan to dark brown, often masked with algae or mud, bears three rows of weak to prominent keels, and is serrated toward the back. The lower shell, or plastron, is yellow to tan, un-patterned, relatively small, and cross-shaped in outline. The snapper's tail is as long as the carapace, with saw-toothed keels running down the top. Wild specimens weigh up to 45 pounds. Some fattened captives exceed 75 pounds. Snappers have massive heads with powerful, hooked jaws. They strike viciously when lifted from water or teased, and can inflict a serious bite. That being said, the snapping turtle's demeanor in the water is quite different, and there is no credible recorded evidence of a snapping turtle biting anybody while in the water. Indeed, if this were not so, people would be bitten left and right.

Subspecies include the eastern snapping turtle (*C. s. serpentina*), which is characterized by the blunt tubercles on the neck and is present throughout most of its range, except Florida; and the Florida snapping turtle (*C. s. osceola*), which has pointed tubercles on the neck and is present throughout the Florida peninsula.

Breeding occurs April to November with peak laying season in June. The female lays as many as 83 (typically 25 to 50) spherical, 1⅛-inch (29-millimeter) eggs in roughly a 4-foot 7-inch- (10- to 18-centimeter-) deep, flask-shaped cavity. Each egg is directed into place by alternating movements of the hind feet. Incubation, depending on weather, takes 9 to 18 weeks. In temperate localities, hatchlings overwinter in the nest. Females may retain sperm for several years. Females often travel to a nesting site some distance from water.

In general, snapping turtle habitat is fresh water. They like soft mud bottoms and abundant vegetation. They can also be found in brackish waters.

Their range is southern Alberta to Nova Scotia, south to the Gulf. These turtles are highly aquatic; they like to rest in warm shallows, often buried in mud, with only the eyes and nostrils exposed. They emerge in April from a winter retreat beneath an overhanging mud bank, under vegetative debris, or inside a muskrat lodge. The snapper eats invertebrates, carrion, aquatic plants, fish, birds, and small mammals. It is an excellent swimmer: individuals displaced 2 miles have returned to their capture sites within several hours.

Snapping Turtles

Almost 30 years ago, my fishing partner Ron and I sat by a small campfire on the banks of Oak Orchard Creek in Orleans County, New York. We were 2 days on the river, bass fishing in a small skiff and pitching a little pup tent at night when we got tired. When you're old enough to focus on something and young enough to go without much sleep, fishing can be a pretty serious affair. After 14 hours of casting for bass, any sane person would crawl into bed and call it a day. Naturally, we broke out the worm rigs and bobbers and commenced night fishing. Plenty of time to sleep later!

The trick was to float your bobber far enough out to where you thought a nice bullhead or channel catfish lay, but close enough so you could still make out your bobber in the firelight. I had one small bullhead on a nylon cord stringer. My scheme was to get at least two fish for breakfast the next morning, but after a half hour of no nibbles, I reeled my worm in and went to check on my fish. I remarked to myself that it felt a good deal lighter hauling it in than when I had put it out. I smiled as I saw the fish's head come into view in the firelight. I pulled up the stringer in order to tease my fishing buddy who had not caught anything that evening. My smile quickly faded when I realized that all that remained of my fish was just that—its head! Something had bitten off the entire fish from the head back. After our initial shock, my partner thought it was pretty funny. He proceeded to make some lame wisecrack about the rare "big-headed catfish" that lurked in these waters. As I sat there broken-hearted, trying desperately to think of some snappy comeback, some movement in the shallows caught my attention.

Under the dim campfire light, the huge turtle looked like some weird kind of aquatic dinosaur as he slowly came into view in the shallow water. The length of his top shell, or carapace, looked to be in excess of 20 inches as I watched the highest points on his back quietly dimple the surface. His head was easily the size of my outstretched hand. Four thick, stocky legs that terminated in blunt claws and a stegosaurus-like tail completed his prehistoric demeanor as he searched the shallows for food. We sat quietly in the dark admiring his size and were thankful for the visit that lent some excitement to an otherwise slow night of angling. Suddenly, he stopped and appeared to touch his nose to something on the mud bottom. Something was wiggling in front of his nose.

It dawned on me too late that I had left my baited hook hanging in the water. I got the word uh-oh out of my mouth just as the big snapper inhaled my bait. I grabbed the rod, thinking that all I would do now would make it worse, but I also knew that the large reptile was capable of either snapping my rod or stripping all the line off the reel—neither scenario pleased me.

Rather than pull upward and risk driving the hook into the roof of his mouth, I instantly decided to sweep the rod parallel to the ground and give it a couple of good, hard tugs. To this day, I don't know who was more surprised when the hook came free, me or the turtle. He stared for a moment in the direction his intended snack had leapt out of the water, then slowly turned himself around and headed out into deep water. I now know that if need be, I can cut the line as close as possible to the turtle, and the hook will be broken down by rust and the turtle's own body chemistry, quicker than most people think.

Turtles Crossing Highways

Most species of turtles begin their reproductive behavior sometime in the spring. This can vary depending on the latitude. In spring and early summer, it is common to see turtles of any species crossing highways in search of a suitable place to lay their eggs, often in some form of soft earth a good distance from any obvious water. The reason for this is so that the egg site does not become flooded from any high water conditions that may occur. The female turtle chooses a site that will be warmed by the sun and begins digging and scooping the dirt with her hind legs. This can often take a couple hours. Once finished with the excavation, she will deposit a number of eggs in the hole and cover them by pushing the dirt back over the eggs. After egg-laying, she will return to the water and the eggs are left alone.

Where we humans get involved is with our concern for the turtle being run over in the road. This is certainly an appropriate instance in which to help, but we need to provide the right kind of intervention. One of the most important things to remember when moving a turtle or any animal off the highway is personal safety. It is never a good idea to jeopardize human life to save an animal in trouble. Attempting a rescue in busy traffic is just not worth the risk.

Once we address the safety issues, the next thing to keep in mind is that the turtle must always be moved off the road in the direction it is going. The reason for this is that the egg-laying behavior of turtles is a very hardwired instinct. Turn a turtle around and point it in the other direction, and more often than not, it will eventually turn right around and go back in the direction it was going in the first place. Moving it off the road in the same direction assures that we are not intervening in a way that could put the animal at risk all over again.

Actually getting the turtles off the highway can be easy. The smaller basking species, such as sliders and painted turtles, can simply be picked up by the back portion of their shell and either moved to the side of the road or, if too heavy, placed in a container. Snapping turtles require a little more care in handling. Small snappers can be picked up by the rear portion of their shells safely by first drawing an imaginary line crossways across the shell between the front and rear legs. Then anywhere you can get a grip behind that line will keep you out of reach of their long neck. Another great way to move a bigger snapper is to get a short length of rope or old towel and hang it in front of the snapper's nose. Its pugnacious temperament will usually cause it to bite the towel. Gently drag it off the road and then come back later for the towel.

WHAT..Is That?

I get the same call every year. *"There's a beaver in my backyard..."*

Many people are not as familiar with the woodchuck as they are with other more recognizable animals like raccoons or squirrels. Once thought of as just a creature of country meadows and farmlands, the woodchuck, or groundhog, is now a familiar sight in town. Before someone asks the inevitable question: hey, how much wood can a woodchuck chuck? (Sigh...) The name woodchuck actually comes from a Cree Indian word, wuchak, used to identify several different animals of similar size and color, including other marmots; it has nothing to do with the woodchuck's habits or habitat. So the correct answer to the proverbial question is none.

Belonging to the squirrel family of rodents, it is stout with short legs and a short, bushy tail. The woodchuck is a grizzled brown with color variations from red to black. Its size can range from 2 pounds to as much as 15 pounds. Although its traditional habitat includes pastures, meadows, and wooded areas, the green space provided in many suburban housing areas can fit the bill nicely. Large burrows with mounds of dirt outside the main entrance, plus additional secondary escape exits, are tip-offs that a chuck has taken residence. Woodchucks feed on grasses like clover, alfalfa, and winter wheat. They are also fond of corn and other agricultural crops.

This sun-loving creature is active by day, especially in the early morning and late afternoon. With the exception of the far West Coast, woodchucks are native to most of the United States. In late summer or early fall, the woodchuck puts on a heavy layer of fat, which sustains it through hibernation. It digs a winter burrow with a hibernation chamber, where it curls up in a ball on a mat of grasses. The animal's body temperature falls from almost 97 to less than 40 degrees Fahrenheit (36 to 4 degrees Celsius), its breathing slows to once every 6 minutes, and its heartbeat drops from more than 100 beats per minute to 4.

There are those rare instances when chucks can do damage in a garden and will also burrow under sheds and porches much like a skunk. In moderate numbers, woodchucks are actually beneficial. Their digging aerates and loosens the soil, and their defecation fertilizes it. Chucks are responsible for transforming over a million tons of subsoil into valuable topsoil in New York State annually.

Because of the woodchuck's tendency to get rather large, many homeowners are concerned when they discover a chuck in their backyard. What makes matters worse is that woodchucks, like other urban species, can get rather relaxed with us and sometimes don't hightail it back to their burrow right away, which makes many of us a little nervous about the big roly-poly ground squirrel waddling about the yard.

A woodchuck's main defense is its eyesight. This is why you will see them periodically stand up on their hind legs to get a better view of their surroundings.

Largely unmolested by natural predators in the suburbs, woodchucks tend to lose their skittish behavior and become a little more blasé toward humans. This behavior is nothing for us to be concerned about. More often than not, when we choose to use the backyard, the woodchuck will opt out and return to its hole, particularly if the family dog shows up. Most chucks will give any dog a wide berth, and it takes a particularly agile or cunning pooch to be able to consistently cut off a woodchuck's escape route. Be advised, however, that a cornered woodchuck is capable of defending itself and will not come quietly. Left alone, they are rarely a problem and can actually be quite entertaining to watch.

Woodchucks have one litter of four or five young per year, born from April through early May, after a 28-day gestation. Blind and naked at birth, they open their eyes and crawl at about 1 month and disperse at 2 months.

Woodchucks can be excluded with some of the methods described in the section on habitat modification. A good trick to help keep them out of the garden is a chicken wire fence. Bend it into an L shape with the bottom leg lying on the ground facing out. Stake that part down if needed. The secret for the vertical portion is to not pull it taught between the stakes. Leaving it a little loose will make the chuck uncomfortable in climbing it. Chucks can climb, but they're not particularly agile. The loose, wobbly chicken wire often discourages them from scaling the fence. If they are not impacting vegetation or interfering with drainage, chucks can be left to their own devices with little worry. They are often not the easiest animals to livetrap, and so, removal should be carefully considered before hiring any professional help.

Simply put, a zoonotic disease is a disease that can be transmitted from animals to people. It is a subject that can be very vast in content and detail. There are entire books written on this topic. I have included some of the more common diseases that many people ask about, and that the average person might want to keep in mind. It is surprising to me the numbers of people who, I believe, are overly concerned about contracting diseases from wildlife. Most of the time, any inherent risk of contacting disease from wildlife is already mitigated through common sense and good hygiene.

Giardiasis

Giardiasis is caused by a protozoan called giardia. It is transmitted through contaminated water. The disease is characterized by headache, flatulence, diarrhea, and abdominal pain. Certain wildlife species can spread giardia when they are in contact with the source of the contamination. One example of a contamination risk would be raccoons that can often foul standing water when attracted to a property regularly. For instance, kiddie pools or ornamental ponds can be at risk when raccoons are being fed nearby. Ponds created by beaver dams can also be a classic source of giardia exposure for the family dog.

Salmonellosis

Caused by a bacterium called salmonella, this is another enteric disease that can cause headache, nausea, diarrhea, and blood poisoning. Transmission is usually through the fecal-oral route facilitated by improper hygiene. Birds and reptiles can be major carriers of this disease. As always, common sense should prevail here, with children and adults washing their hands after contact with these types of animals. It is recommended that very young children, the elderly, or those with compromised immune systems refrain from handling reptiles regularly. In addition, no reptile, captive or wild, should have any contact with any surface in the kitchen. Zoonotic diseases can be a concern, but as with all wildlife issues, it is a thoughtful approach and common sense that should be foremost in our minds.

West Nile Virus

First identified in the 1930s, this disease emerged in North America in the late 1990s. In the relatively few cases of human exposure, the disease manifests itself as a form of encephalitis. At present there are over 138 species of birds and mammals that have been detected to carry the virus. Corvids, which include crows and jays, were the first birds to be labeled as indicator species. Birds of prey were not far behind, with owls being particularly susceptible. The disease is primarily transmitted by mosquitoes to both birds and people, but it has also been isolated in other types of insects. Much is still being learned about this virus and the way it affects wildlife. There has been no proven direct transmission from animals to humans, and at this time, nothing like that should be assumed. The most effective action that should be taken by us is the removal of any stagnant standing water on our property. Water in bird baths should be changed once a week, and any debris or trash that can harbor breeding mosquitoes should be thrown out. These simple-to-follow recommendations will decrease the mosquito population, helping to protect both you and the birds in your neighborhood. Local branches of county health departments are capable of answering specific questions and providing up-to-the-minute information to area residents.

Lyme disease

First recorded in the town of Lyme, Connecticut, this disease is transmitted through the bite of an infected tick of the genus *Ixodes* or deer tick. Only certain individuals of that species can be infected with a microscopic organism that causes the disease. The organism is called *Borellia burgdorferi* and belongs to a larger family of disease-causing agents called spirochetes. Wearing long pants and socks while hiking in heavy brush where ticks are known to exist can drastically reduce exposure to this disease. Also, thoroughly inspecting our dogs after hiking in the tall grass can often prevent tick bites. Lyme disease in humans and animals can be signaled by low-grade fever, general malaise, transient lameness, and irregular heartbeat. The site of a tick bite on humans is often, but not always, indicated by a round, raised bulls-eye rash. The disease can be difficult to detect but fairly easy to treat with the appropriate antibiotics. Specific pet-related questions can be answered by a veterinarian.

Rabies

As with most wildlife issues, the subject of rabies is one that should be treated with proper education, facts, and common sense. Rabies is a virus that is normally transmitted through the bite of an infective animal. There are other, less well-known routes of transmission such as inhalation scenarios in caves with large amounts of dried bat guano, etc., but animal bites are the most common. Unlike other viruses, rabies migrates along the nervous system rather than through the bloodstream. This can cause unusually long incubation periods before the onset of disease symptoms.

Rabies can manifest itself in two basic forms: furious and dumb. Furious rabies can be seen as distinctly abnormal and/or aggressive behavior, salivation, and tremors. Dumb rabies is usually seen as being absent of any obvious signs, other than perhaps abnormally quiet or tame behavior. In addition, rabies is often called "the great imitator" with respect to making a visual diagnosis because the neurological signs are often mistaken for canine distemper.

For example, where I live in New York State, there are currently three species of animals that are classified as rabies vector species (RVS): the raccoon, the bat, and the skunk. This does not mean that all of the individuals of these species are infected with rabies; it merely means that the disease is currently being found in, and has adapted itself for a time to, those species. This equates to a common-sense approach for us when we encounter these animals. Direct contact is never advisable. We recommend a call to a qualified wildlife rehabilitator for advice when there is a question of possible disease. In addition, the local branch of the health department should be notified in the event of any direct handling of a rabies vector animal, regardless of whether it is exhibiting signs of rabies. All bats found within the living space of a home should be reported to the local health department.

Sarcoptes Scabiei (Mange or Scabies)

Sarcoptic mange is the name for the skin disease caused by infection with the *Sarcoptes scabiei* mite. Mites are not insects; instead, they are more closely related to spiders. They are microscopic and cannot be seen with the naked eye.

Adult *Sarcoptes scabiei* mites live 3 to 4 weeks in the host's skin. After mating, the female burrows into the skin depositing three to four eggs in the tunnel behind her. The eggs hatch in 3 to 10 days, producing a larva that, in turn, moves about on the skin surface, eventually molting into a nymphal stage, and finally into an adult. The adults move on the surface of the skin where they mate, and the cycle begins again with the female burrowing and laying eggs.

The presence of a female sarcoptes mite burrowing in the skin and leaving a trail of eggs behind her generates an inflammatory response in the skin similar to an allergic response. The motion of the mite in and on the skin is extremely itchy. Further, the presence of mites and their eggs generates a massive allergic response in the skin that is even itchier.

The term scabies refers to mite infestations by either *Sarcoptes scabiei* or other mite species closely related to *Sarcoptes scabiei*. While *Sarcoptes scabiei* can infect humans and cats, it tends not to persist on these hosts. When people (including some veterinarians) refer to sarcoptic mange, or scabies, in the cat, they are usually referring to infection by *Notoedres cati*, a mite closely related to *Sarcoptes scabiei*. In these feline cases, it would be more correct to refer to *notoedric* mange, though the treatment for both mites is the same. *Notoedric mange* in cats generally produces facial itching and scabbing. In humans scabies produces itching, redness, and scabbing. But again, it is a self-limiting condition in humans, usually requiring nothing more than possible treatment for the temporary uncomfortable effects.

Ringworm

What is ringworm? Well, ringworm is not a worm at all.

Ringworm is a contagious fungus infection that can affect the scalp, the body, the feet (athlete's foot), or the nails.

People can get ringworm from direct skin-to-skin contact with an infected person or pet, indirect contact with an object or surface that an infected person or pet has touched, or rarely, by contact with soil.

Ringworm can be treated with fungus-killing medicine.

To prevent ringworm, make sure all infected persons and pets get appropriate treatment. Plus, avoid contact with infected persons and pets. Do not share personal items such as combs, and keep common-use areas clean.

Ringworm is caused by several different fungus organisms that all belong to a group called *dermatophytes*. Different dermatophytes affect different parts of the body and cause the various types of ringworm: ringworm of the scalp, ringworm of the body, ringworm of the foot (athlete's foot), and ringworm of the nails.

Ringworm is widespread around the world and in the United States. The fungus that causes scalp ringworm lives in humans and animals. The fungus that causes ringworm of the body lives in humans, animals, and soil. The fungi that cause ringworm of the foot and ringworm of the nails live only in humans.

Ringworm of the scalp usually begins as a small pimple that becomes larger, leaving scaly patches of temporary baldness. Infected hairs become brittle and break off easily. Yellowish crusty areas sometimes develop. Infections elsewhere on the body show up as a flat, round patch anywhere on the skin except for the scalp and feet. The groin is a common area of infection (groin ringworm). As the rash gradually expands, its center clears to produce a ring. More than one patch might appear, and the patches can overlap. The area is sometimes itchy.

Ringworm of the foot is also called athlete's foot. It appears as a scaling or cracking of the skin, especially between the toes.

Ringworm of the nails causes the affected nails either to become thicker, discolored, and brittle, or to become chalky and disintegrate.

Scalp ringworm usually appears 10 to 14 days after contact and ringworm of the skin 4 to 10 days after contact. The time between exposure and symptoms is not known for the other types of ringworm.

A health-care provider can diagnose the disease by examining the site of infection with special tests. Anyone can get ringworm. Scalp ringworm often strikes young children; outbreaks have been recognized in schools, day-care centers, and infant nurseries. School athletes are at risk for scalp ringworm, ringworm of the body, and foot ringworm; there have been outbreaks among high school wrestling teams. Children with young pets are at increased risk for ringworm of the body.

Ringworm can be treated with fungus-killing medicine. The medicine can be taken in tablet or liquid form by mouth, or as a cream applied directly to the affected area. Lack of or inadequate treatment can result in an infection that will not clear up.

Although ringworm is not tracked by health authorities, infections appear to be increasing steadily, especially among pre-school and school-age children. Early recognition and treatment are needed to slow the spread of infection and to prevent reinfection.

Chapter 28 - "Tails" of the Bizarre

After putting the majority of this book together, it occurred to me that there were some writings that didn't really seem to fit with the rest of the book. My first reaction was to put them aside, but after thinking it over, I decided to actually jot down one or two more and devise a separate chapter: "Tails" of the Bizarre. Clever huh?

I couldn't really leave any of them out as they are, each in their own way, weird little windows into who I am, what I do, and how animal people never really get away from the world we live in.

As a shelter worker, vet tech, falconer, naturalist, and hunter, the line between my professional and my private life gets a little blurry now and then. Animals do what they do, and anyone believing that they have them all figured out is either kidding us or kidding themselves.

A Fish Story

Before our daughter was born, my wife and I spent a great deal of time fishing. I take all the credit for introducing her to the sport, and she takes all the credit for routinely out-fishing me. It's bad enough when something like that happens, but when someone does it while doing everything "wrong," it just adds insult to injury.

I attempted to give my spouse a well-rounded introduction to all the mysteries and techniques of angling passed down to me during my youth, and perfected through countless hours on the water. She responded by giving credence to the old saying "a little knowledge is a dangerous thing." The fact that

*her antics regularly put fish on the stringer is of little conse-
quence. Any experienced angler will tell you that there are
rules of etiquette and protocol that must be strictly adhered to
while in pursuit of fish. It's what separates us from the animals. It prevents complete anarchy, perhaps even mutiny,
aboard ship.*

*Our first lessons involved the use of live bait such as worms
or minnows. In the interests of chivalry and expediency, I took
charge of baiting her hook. I must say she did progress rapidly. I rewarded her studiousness by slowly unveiling the world
of artificial lures to her. I remember the gleam in her eye when
the realization took hold that impaling some small, squirmy,
smelly creature onto a hook was now theoretically unnecessary. It was here that the time-honored teacher-student relationship began to break down. She began pawing through my
secret and deadly array of spoons, plugs, and spinners, occasionally asking silly, yet adorable questions about certain
items. And then it happened. She discovered the box of soft
plastic worms and grubs. Myriad shapes, sizes, and colors,
most with curly tails that produced a swimming motion in the
water. I had every intention of teaching her that particular art,
but all in due time.*

*My fishing partner suddenly cast aside, if you will, all the
principles and techniques I had taught her and immediately
began all sorts of embarrassing experimentation with different
combinations of plastic baits and odd riggings. All of them
were absolutely wrong. I began looking over my shoulder to
make sure there were no other boats anchored near enough to
perceive the silly and ridiculous offerings she was pitching
over the side of the boat. Spinners on backwards, and jigs
attached with giant snap swivels rather than tied neatly to*

the end of her line. I gently tried to voice my disapproval without crushing her spirit, but to no avail.

Finally, after rummaging around in my tackle box, she came up with a particularly ridiculous looking combination: a tiny pink ice fishing jig (I immediately pointed out that we were not ice fishing) baited with a small pink plastic grub, and once again attached to her line by means of a large snap swivel of the kind normally used to rig up a large bass plug. Nice looking earring, I smirked to myself as she watched it fluttering beneath the surface next to the boat. Having given up, for the time being, trying to teach her correct techniques, I vowed to let her flail the water for a few hours in a vain attempt to catch something. Whenever she decided to demonstrate the right amount of contrition, I would then consider assisting her.

I heard her gasp from her end of the canoe that she had "got something." I sighed as I put my rod down in preparation to again remove her terminal tackle from some submerged log or other underwater obstacle. As I glanced over my shoulder to see exactly where she was hung up, I saw her rod bent over in that unmistakable vibrating arc that meant a fish was on the other end. As I turned in my seat to try to get a better look, her rod tip disappeared under the water, and the drag on her reel began to whine.

The northern pike that was doing its best to pull her over the side looked as long as my leg, as it made short runs back and forth under the canoe. The fish stopped intermittently to shake its big head back and forth in an effort to dislodge the hook; its huge jaws, full of teeth, were easy to make out in the clear water of the Adirondack lake. She did a good job playing the big fish, and once we had it securely on the stringer, we decided to head back to camp to clean our catch and get some lunch. As we paddled across the lake, she could only contain herself for so long, and eventually she asked me what I though of her new invention. Naturally, I stated the obvious and pointed out how, sooner or later, anything would catch fish if used long enough. Then I added that she was lucky enough to encounter a dumb specimen that was obviously muddying the gene pool.

As I rummaged through my bag to retrieve a granola bar, I noticed that I had a few more of those little pink plastic grubs. I silently wondered if I had any more of those ice fishing jigs...

Why I'm still a little afraid of the dark

I went through that phase like all kids do, I guess. Like checking under the bed, freaking out at little noises, and so on. My light switch was on the other side of the room from my bed, obviously a sick joke perpetrated by my father, who had built our house. I can remember perfecting the flying leap under the covers from across the room after flicking the switch off. But every kid grows up, and I eventually got a handle on the idea that there was nothing in the dark that could ever hurt me. I labored under that delusion for many years.

It was one of those mornings a bow hunter waits for—cold and crisp, with a very light breeze. I cut cross-wind through the early morning gloom, parallel to my tree stand, and once downwind, turned into the breeze and started sneaking into my hunting spot. As I stepped off the soft dirt of the open plowed crop field and into the brush, I heard the unmistakable sound of a deer jumping up from its bed and crashing away from me through the frost-covered goldenrod. Instinctively, I flipped on the flashlight I always have in my pocket and scanned the field where the noise originated. I imme-

diately picked up the shape of a fat little four-point buck about 40 yards away as he slowed to a walk, apparently feeling safe in the darkness from whatever had disturbed him. I smiled to myself as I watched him under the soft glow of the flashlight. I knew he wasn't all that upset. I also noted that he was dead upwind from me, and so, I was hoping to see him later on after sunrise.

I was just about to click the light off and finish slipping over to my stand, when the buck stopped and looked my way. I figured the jig was up and that the deer, suddenly realizing that it was being observed, would bug out real quick. Instead, he turned and began walking directly toward me.

My initial reaction at this turn of events was one of amusement. It was during the rut, and deer sometimes did seemingly silly things during the peak of their breeding season. More than one buck has been converted to steaks because of it. I stood there in the dark, bow in one hand, flashlight in the other, and a quiver of arrows on my back, waiting for the confused whitetail to realize his mistake. He didn't. The wind was blowing from his direction right to me, so he was unable to detect any of my human scent. When he closed the distance to about 30 yards, I muttered under my breath some empty threat involving how I'd like to see him do that if I were holding a gun.

At 25 yards or so, he showed no sign of a clue or of slowing down, so I spoke to him quietly but firmly, secure in the knowledge that the sound of my voice would snap him back to reality. "Hey you," I said for lack of a snappier line. What do you say to a dazed, lovesick deer you meet in the dark? Spare me what you're thinking; I've recounted this tale enough to be able to read your mind. I can tell this story today and laugh. I *can assure you that at the time, in the dark, it was anything but funny.*

At around 15 yards, I began backing up and intermittently sort of hissing at the deer as he closed the remaining distance between us, all the while fully expecting the big dope to get it together and vanish before my eyes. Looking back, it is still very weird and surreal to me. All deer hunters spend their entire careers being quiet in the woods, and although this certainly was rapidly beginning to qualify as a time to make some real noise, all I could think of to do was to make these shooing noises as I tried to increase the distance between us, all the while not wanting to turn my back on him.

At maybe 12 feet or so, my animal handling and control training took over. I placed the closest thing at hand between me and the animal, and that was my compound bow. By now I had decided that the last thing I wanted to do was touch him, but I still wanted something between us. I had no clue what was going on in his little pea brain, but I knew he had no idea I was a human. In my head, I began to go over the various scenarios that might occur. If we made contact and he mistook me for another buck, I knew I could be seriously injured. If he figured out what I was, I could still be injured depending on what he decided to do. Although I was just 200 or 300 yards from civilization, it might as well have been 2 or 3 miles. Oddly, I also thought how this could be a real dumb way to die.

I had backed up into a dense thicket as far as I could, and by now I could clearly see the dazed expression on the deer's face as he literally walked right up to me. I had kept my bow between us but had pulled it in toward my body as the deer backed me into the thicket, not wanting to be the one that triggered whatever it was that was sure to come next. I could clearly see and hear the deer's breath as he craned his neck forward in an attempt to gather any kind of information he could, his face and antlers fully illuminated and inches from my chest.

If this were a TV movie, it's here that they usually cut to a commercial.

Okay, okay, we'll keep going.

Just as I thought he would stick his big wet nose up against my chest, the breeze swirled ever so slightly. Suddenly he snorted, wheeled around, and dashed back the way he came from, making huge 15-foot leaps through the brush. I declined to monitor his progress and immediately beat feet for my ladder stand set up on the edge of a nearby thicket. I closed the 35 yards to the thicket in seconds. As I reached the thicket, it dawned on me that I no longer heard the deer crashing through the frozen brush. Instinctively I stopped to listen, assuming the deer had left the area. Just as I went to slip into the cover where my tree stand was concealed, I heard him walking—back toward me. I was fairly certain I could get to the stand but that didn't help much. I was pretty shook-up as I climbed the ladder stand and onto the platform. With shaking hands, I hung my pack and quiver, and clipped my safety belt to the tree. A moment later, the familiar footsteps began again, and in the gloom I could just make out the shape of the buck as he appeared below me, nose to the ground and right on my trail.

Safe in my stand, my fear began to turn to annoyance. I watched the buck circle the clearing below in an attempt to find me, apparently still not convinced of what I was. I am and have been, for all of my adult life, a pretty law-abiding guy, particularly when it comes to game laws and hunting regulations. It was a good solid 20 minutes before legal shooting time. And I could see him, but not well enough to take an ethically acceptable shot, even at the close range he was pacing around at. A thought occurred to me. I reached into my pocket and found my deer call. Adjusting the reed to reproduce a doe bleat, I bleated softly at the buck still milling aimlessly around my tree stand. It had the desired effect as he immediately began pacing around in earnest, now convinced he had let the opportunity of a lifetime slip through his fingers (or more accurately, his hooves). This went on for at least 10 minutes with the young buck convinced he would find the "doe" any second.

Daylight was gathering momentum, and I slipped an arrow out of the quiver and nocked it on the bowstring. As he came into view again, his head passed behind a sapling, blocking his line of site to me. Just as I began to draw my bow, a clattering sound split the quiet morning, and the buck's head snapped up looking toward the sound. It took a couple of seconds to process what I was hearing. It was the sound of deer antlers clashing together. Suddenly the buck folded his tent, broke camp, and was gone in a flash. Not only did I not see him again that week of the rut, but I never saw that particular deer again that season.

To this day, I don't know if the young buck thought he was about to get his butt kicked by one or more larger bucks, or if he figured out what I did later that morning. And that was that another hunter had slipped into my area, unaware of my presence, and began the process of rattling or clashing deer antlers together, simulating a fight between two bucks in order to call in a curious deer. The technique does not work all the time, but when it does, the results can be dramatic. One of the downsides can be that smaller bucks will often react negatively to the sound and leave the area.

This encounter happened over a decade ago, and I have since hunted the same land year after year without ever having had an experience like that again.

I know that it was a convergence of many variables that led to that strange encounter that morning: time of year, wind direction, my own strict scent control habits, etc. I still bow hunt and my habit is to still get in my stands early, before daylight. But between you and me, to this day it's still not quite the same as before. I'm a little antsy on my way into the woods these days. Just a little.

Epilogue

It has been said that it's impossible to stick your toes into a river twice in the same place. Since the river is constantly moving, that place is only "there" for an instant and then it is gone. Rivers flow, the land changes, and time inevitably marches on.

We are forever changing the face of our world, and, as time passes by, more and more people are finding themselves living closer and closer to the wild creatures we share this planet with. And so, along with this, the challenge grows. The challenge to keep finding ways to live peacefully and thoughtfully next door to animals who have no choice but to try and adapt themselves to constantly changing—and often shrinking—habitats. In this, they have no choice, for it is the way they are made. We, however, have the divine gift of reason and the freedom of choice. We can decide that wild things are important to us; they're vital to our existence in ways we haven't yet realized, and as such, deserve a place in our lives and in our neighborhoods.

The book of Proverbs says that "a righteous man regardeth the life of his beast." Within this simple verse we are provided as much room for choices as we have relationships with animals, and we have been afforded many types of relationships. Some are cooperative, some symbiotic, and others, purely esthetic. Whether around the home or through the hunt, by virtue of feeding them or being fed by them, we have an obligation to always try and make the best decisions possible in every situation. That much we do owe as responsible stewards of this incredible gift of wildlife.

About the Author

Joel Thomas was born and raised in East Amherst, just north of Buffalo, New York. He grew up spending most of his free time outdoors. A childhood interest in animals and wildlife eventually led to work in the late 70's as an assistant keeper for one of the largest private reptile collections in Western New York. He graduated from Medaille College in 1993 with a degree in veterinary technology. He has worked at the Erie County SPCA as a veterinary technician since 1995 and became Wildlife Administrator there in 1999. He is a New York State Licensed Veterinary Technician, a Wildlife Rehabilitator, and a Falconer. He also holds certifications in chemical capture and as a New York State DEC Hunter Education Instructor.

Joel lives in rural Niagara Country, NY with his wife Tracy, daughter Hannah, a couple hawks and Sam...the wonder dog.

For further information about this book and the author visit
www.creaturecomfortsbook.com or www.amazon.com

6600467R0

Made in the USA
Charleston, SC
11 November 2010